"Rare is the resource that brings toge. sensitivity and relevance. That's why I'm delighted to see the launch of the Essential Studies in Biblical Theology series. Each volume expounds a central biblical-theological theme in a way that helps pastors, students, and laypeople alike not lose the forest of Scripture's overarching story line from the trees of its myriad of motifs and subplots. And what better way to kick off such a promising series than with Benjamin Gladd's fine study of the nature of the people of God from Genesis to Revelation through the lens of being in God's image. Highly recommend!"

Todd Wilson, president of the Center for Pastor Theologians

"The main storyline and big message of the Bible can be told from many different angles. Benjamin Gladd's book takes a surprising approach, insisting that not only is Jesus God's prophet, priest, and king—we too, as those created in God's image and being conformed to the image of Christ, are to live as prophets, priests, and kings. The book is a remarkably comprehensive and compelling description of God's work in the world."

Brian S. Rosner, principal, Ridley College, Australia

"An ambitious undertaking that makes an immense amount of biblical theology accessible to readers at any level. Gladd's study of the people of God is clearly grounded in the biblical text, uses covenant theology with a light but precise touch, and seamlessly integrates practical application. Despite its focus on a single theme, it integrates numerous other themes along the way, and so is almost a whole-Bible theology in miniature."

Daniel Timmer, professor of biblical studies, Puritan Reformed Theological Seminary, and professeur d'Ancien Testament, Faculté de Théologie Évangélique, Montréal

"In this concise, clear book Ben Gladd helps us understand the crucial connections between image of God and the roles of prophet, priest, and king. Gladd masterfully guides us through the Bible to see how Jesus, the true Israel, embodies and models these roles, which are now the calling of his church. I highly recommend this book as a guide for putting the whole Bible together with Jesus at the center."

Chris Bruno, associate dean and assistant professor of New Testament and biblical theology at Bethlehem College & Seminary

"From Genesis to Revelation, Benjamin Gladd deftly guides the reader through Scripture and unpacks the rich mosaic of the people of God. Giving attention to various canonical themes such as temple, image, Israel, king, priest, and prophet, Gladd not only shows how Christ fulfills them but also how the church—as the people of God in Christ—lives before him. Even those who disagree with some aspects of Gladd's approach will be encouraged and challenged to 'develop new creational patterns' of living now while waiting for the not yet, when Christ comes again to make all things new."

Oren R. Martin, assistant professor of Christian theology at The Southern Baptist Theological Seminary and Boyce College

FROM ADAM AND ISRAEL
TO THE CHURCH
A Biblical Theology
of the People of God

BENJAMIN L. GLADD

Academic
An imprint of InterVarsity Press
Downers Grove, Illinois

InterVarsity Press
P.O. Box 1400, Downers Grove, IL 60515-1426
ivpress.com
email@ivpress.com

InterVarsity Press® is the book-publishing division of InterVarsity Christian Fellowship/USA®, a movement of students and faculty active on campus at hundreds of universities, colleges, and schools of nursing in the United States of America, and a member movement of the International Fellowship of Evangelical Students. For information about local and regional activities, visit intervarsity.org.

All Scripture quotations, unless otherwise indicated, are taken from The Holy Bible, New International Version®, NIV®. Copyright © 1973, 1978, 1984, 2011 by Biblica, Inc.™ Used by permission of Zondervan. All rights reserved worldwide. www.zondervan.com. The "NIV" and "New International Version" are trademarks registered in the United States Patent and Trademark Office by Biblica, Inc.™

Cover design and image composite: David Fassett
Interior design: Daniel van Loon
Image: vector pattern: © Samolevsky / iStock / Getty Images Plus

ISBN 978-0-8308-5543-8 (print)
ISBN 978-0-8308-5544-5 (digital)

Printed in the United States of America ♾

Library of Congress Cataloging-in-Publication Data
Names: Gladd, Benjamin L., author.
Title: From Adam and Israel to the church : a biblical theology of the people of God / Benjamin L. Gladd.
Description: Downers Grove, Illinois : IVP Academic, an imprint of InterVarsity Press, [2019] |
    Series: Essential studies in biblical theology | Includes bibliographical references and index.
Identifiers: LCCN 2019036658 (print) | LCCN 2019036659 (ebook) | ISBN 9780830855438 (paperback) |
    ISBN 9780830855445 (ebook)
Subjects: LCSH: People of God—Biblical teaching. | Jesus Christ—Person and offices. | God
    (Christianity)—Worship and love. | Church—Biblical teaching.
Classification: LCC BS680.P43 G53 2019 (print) | LCC BS680.P43 (ebook) | DDC 262/.7—dc23
LC record available at https://lccn.loc.gov/2019036658
LC ebook record available at https://lccn.loc.gov/2019036659

P   25   24   23   22   21   20   19   18   17   16   15   14   13   12   11   10   9   8   7   6   5   4   3   2   1

Y   37   36   35   34   33   32   31   30   29   28   27   26   25   24   23   22   21   20   19

To Nikki, Judah, and Simon

CONTENTS

SERIES PREFACE

THE ESSENTIAL STUDIES IN BIBLICAL THEOLOGY is pat-
terned after the highly esteemed series New Studies in Biblical Theology, edited
by D. A. Carson. Like the NSBT, this series is devoted to unpacking the various
strands of biblical theology. The field of biblical theology has grown exponen-
tially in recent years, showing no sign of abating. At the heart of biblical theology
is the unfolding nature of God's plan of redemption as set forth in the Bible.

With an influx of so many books on biblical theology, why generate yet
another series? A few reasons. The ESBT is dedicated to the fundamental or
"essential" broad themes of the grand story line of the Bible. Stated succinctly,
the goal of the ESBT is to explore the *central* biblical-theological themes of the
Bible. Several existing series on biblical theology are generally open-ended,
whereas the ESBT will be limited to ten or so volumes. By restricting the entire
series, the scope of the project is established from the beginning. The ESBT
project functions as a whole in that each theme is intentional, and each volume
stands not solely on its own merits. The individual volumes interlock with one
another and, taken together, form a complete and cohesive unit.

Another unique dimension of the series is a robust emphasis on biblical
theology, spanning the entire sweep of the history of redemption. Each volume

traces a particular theme throughout the Bible, from Genesis 1–3 to Revelation 21–22, and is organically connected to the person of Christ and to the New Testament church. To avoid a "flat" biblical theology, these projects are mindful of how the New Testament develops their topic in fresh or unexpected ways. For example, the New Testament sheds new light on the nature of "kingdom" and "messiah." Though these twin themes are rooted and explored in the Old Testament, both flow through the person of Christ in unique ways. Biblical theology should include how Old Testament themes are held in continuity and discontinuity with the New Testament.

The audience of the series includes beginning students of theology, church leaders, and laypeople. The ESBT is intended to be an accessible introduction to core biblical-theological themes of the Bible. This series is not designed to overturn every biblical-theological rock and investigate the finer details of Scripture. Each volume is intentionally brief, serving as a primer of sorts that introduces the reader to a particular theme. These works also attempt to apply their respective biblical-theological themes to Christian living, ministry, and worldview. Good biblical theology warms the heart and motivates us to grow in our knowledge and adoration of the triune God.

Benjamin L. Gladd

AUTHOR'S PREFACE

THIS PROJECT REPRESENTS my own theological journey. Having grown up in a conservative, dispensationalist home and having graduated from The Master's College, I was taught that Israel and the church were two different people groups. Two separate entities with two separate destinies. The church was now living in something of an unexpected parenthesis in the broad story line of the Bible. Predictably, I grew to envy the nation of Israel, as I wanted to inherit *all* of God's promises and fully participate in his program. I didn't want to be a second-class citizen in the people of God.

I went on to study Bible and theology in graduate school, where I learned about "biblical theology" and how the two Testaments properly relate to one another. Israel and the church were not separate but were unified in the person of Christ. Jesus of Nazareth is the true Israel of God, who reconstituted the people of God in himself. So, the church, composed of believing Jews and Gentiles, is the restored people of God, true Israel, because of their identification with him.

A tectonic shift had taken place in how I read the Bible, and one of the things that shaped my understanding was examining the use of the Old Testament in the New. The apostles quote the Old Testament approximately three hundred times and allude to the Old Testament well over a thousand times.

So, when the apostles instruct their congregations, do they plead with them to read the Old Testament as observers or as participants? I believe it's the latter.

This project is, therefore, the fruit of my personal struggle with Israel and the church. Moreover, I've written this book for my students and friends who also are coming to grips with their own identity in Christ. The more I read the New Testament, the more I realize how fundamental this principle was for the early church. The apostles never grew tired of reminding their congregations of working out their identity as the restored people of God and the true Israel.

I'm thankful for my wife, Nikki, and my kids, Judah and Simon, who encourage me beyond measure. My understanding of identity has been sharpened through them. I'm also thankful for my church, Highlands Presbyterian, in Madison, Mississippi, which has given me ample opportunities to teach on this subject. Our friends there warm our hearts toward Christ. I'm thankful for InterVarsity Press for accepting this project. Dan Reid, though now retired, was incredibly encouraging in the initial stages of this project and the ESBT series as a whole. I'm also grateful for Anna Gissing at InterVarsity and her invaluable input. Finally, I'm indebted to Michael Morales and Guy Waters for reading portions of this manuscript and giving me helpful feedback.

Above all, I'm thankful to God, who gave me the desire to pen this project and the energy to complete it. May all glory and honor be his.

To keep the project accessible, my default translation and chapter outlines rely on the New International Version (2011). I often italicize words or phrases within the English translation to demonstrate emphasis or mark parallel wording with the Old Testament. Most of the time these parallels indicate that a New Testament passage is alluding to or quoting the Old Testament.

Benjamin L. Gladd

ABBREVIATIONS

AOAT	Alter Orient und Altes Testament
AUSS	*Andrews University Seminary Studies*
BDAG	*Greek-English Lexicon of the New Testament and Other Early Christian Literature*. Frederick W. Danker, Walter Bauer, William F. Arndt, and F. Wilbur Gingrich. 3rd ed. Chicago: University of Chicago Press, 2000 (Bauer-Danker-Arndt-Gingrich)
BECNT	Baker Exegetical Commentary on the New Testament
BZNW	Beihefte zur Zeitschrift für die neutestamentliche Wissenschaft
CBQ	*Catholic Biblical Quarterly*
COS	*The Context of Scripture*. Edited by William W. Hallo. 3 vols. Leiden: Brill, 1997–2002
IBC	Interpretation: A Bible Commentary for Teaching and Preaching
JETS	*Journal of the Evangelical Theological Society*
JSOTSup	Journal for the Study of the Old Testament Supplement Series
JTISup	Journal for Theological Interpretation, Supplements
NICNT	New International Commentary on the New Testament
NICOT	New International Commentary on the Old Testament
NovTSup	Supplements to Novum Testamentum

NSBT	New Studies in Biblical Theology
PNTC	Pillar New Testament Commentary
TJ	*Trinity Journal*
VTSup	Supplements to Vetus Testamentum
WBC	Word Biblical Commentary
WCF	Westminster Confession of Faith
WUNT	Wissenschaftliche Untersuchungen zum Neuen Testament
ZAW	*Zeitschrift für die alttestamentliche Wissenschaft*
ZECNT	Zondervan Exegetical Commentary on the New Testament

INTRODUCTION

SEVERAL YEARS AGO, I was teaching the Old Testament in a weekly Bible study to a group of college students. A handful of these students were dispensational; that is, they viewed Israel and the church as two separate people groups. At the end of the Bible study, a student came up to me and posed a perceptive question: "If the church and Israel are distinct, then how do I read the Old Testament?" I still remember my answer: "As an observer," I said. But is this how we should read the Old Testament? Is this how Jesus and the apostles read the Scriptures of Israel? As observers? I don't think so. The apostles passionately argued that the church stands in continuity with the people of God in the Old Testament—from Adam to Israel. As such, the church is called to rule over the created order, mediate God's glory to the nations, and embody God's law in every aspect of life.

This volume operates within what theologians call covenant theology. That is, the broad framework of the Bible is organized in accordance with various covenants—the covenant of redemption, covenant of works, and covenant of grace. One cardinal aspect of covenant theology is that the one people of God spans the history of redemption. From Genesis 1–2 to Revelation 21–22, there remains one covenant community. Covenant theology is distinct from dispensational theology. Dispensationalism, a somewhat modern framework, argues that the Bible is organized by distinct dispensations, or strict epochs. At the heart of dispensationalism is the separation between the church and ethnic Israel, that these are distinct people groups and that each functions within its own dispensation.

I intentionally refrain from mapping out all the various strands and permutations of the biblical covenants and how they relate to God and his people within current debates of systematic theology. Contemporary covenant theologians debate the nuances of how the covenants relate to one another in the larger program of the Bible, and there is no need to review such well-trodden ground. What follows, then, is a biblical theology of God's people from the ground up, not top down.

Much of my understanding of the people of God as possessing the divine image stems from G. K. Beale's book *The Temple and the Church's Mission*.[1] Many years ago, that book was seminal to my understanding of the nature of the divine image. So I'm indebted to that volume on a conceptual level. One of Beale's key points is that images are tethered to God's glory in the temple and the larger program of the Bible. In what follows, I will endeavor to sharpen some of these rich insights. Scholars have already written mountain of books on the divine image, and this project makes little attempt to interact with all the literature.

The Bible is filled with wonderful material concerning the divine image and the people of God, but I've restricted my interaction to some of the more prominent passages. In keeping with the goal of the ESBT series, I've skimmed the redemptive-historical cream off the top. I'm only presenting a few of the highlights, so I've tried to resist becoming ensnared in fine exegetical details and engaging scholars at every step. What follows is my attempt to produce an accessible, biblical theology on the people of God and the divine image.

THE NEED FOR THIS STUDY

We all struggle mightily with our identity. Regardless of our age, we long to be part of a group. We want the rights and privileges of a few. We want

---

[1]G. K. Beale, *The Temple and the Church's Mission: A Biblical Theology of the Dwelling Place of God*, NSBT 17 (Downers Grove, IL: InterVarsity Press, 2004).

significance and acceptance. Yet we also want individuality. We want to be treasured for who we are. These age-old pursuits transcend time and culture. These needs are endemic to who we are as humans. The Bible has an incredibly high view of the person, perhaps higher than most Christians realize. In recent years, a movement has been afoot to recognize our dignity and worth. This is especially true in light of the Harvey Weinstein scandal that has swept through Hollywood and taken other industries by storm. Our culture longs to be valued.

The Bible, from Genesis to Revelation, teaches us that humanity is imbued with astonishing qualities. Humanity is the crown of creation. Since we are made in the divine image, we have incredible significance and meaning. The fall certainly perverted how we think and act, but it did not lessen our worth. My prayer is that this project would remind us of our value, who we are in Christ, and what the new creation holds in store for us.

Another reason why I wrote this brief project is to give God's people confidence that they are part of the restored people of God—true Israel. This may seem like only an academic inquiry, but such is not the case.

In 2 Corinthians 6:16-18, for example, the apostle Paul has in mind a number of prominent Old Testament passages as he warns the Gentile Christians:

> What agreement is there between the temple of God and idols?
> For we are the temple of the living God. As God has said:
> "I will live with them
>   and walk among them,
> and I will be their God,
>   and they will be my people."
> Therefore,
> "Come out from them
>   and be separate, says the Lord.
> Touch no unclean thing,
>   and I will receive you."
> And,
> "I will be a Father to you,
>   and you will be my sons and daughters,
>   says the Lord Almighty."

Paul audaciously quotes and alludes to a host of Old Testament texts here—
Leviticus 26, Ezekiel 37, Isaiah 52, Ezekiel 20, and 2 Samuel 7, to name a few.
What's remarkable is that many of these Old Testament texts refer to Israel.
Indeed, the passage from 2 Samuel 7 is a reference to King David! Why would
Paul cite texts that appear to be confined to Israel (and David) and apply
them to a group of Gentiles at Corinth? His words in the next verse (2 Corinthians 7:1) are even more pointed when he claims that "we have these
promises." The Corinthian congregation, a church filled primarily with *Gentile*
Christians, is aligned with Israel, so much so that Paul includes the Corinthians in the lineage of Israel when he tells them the first generation of Israelites are "our ancestors" (1 Corinthians 10:1). Though the Corinthians are
not ethnically part of Israel, they enjoy complete identification with Israel
through their position in Christ, the embodiment of true Israel. The Corinthians must embrace their identity as true Israel and the true temple of God
by not morally compromising. Christian living flows naturally from our
identification as Israel.

THE PURPOSE OF THIS STUDY

The purpose of this book is not to engage with or critique dispensationalism
at every turn. Plenty of books do just that. My project is not polemical. *My
main concern in this project is to examine the nature of the people of God from
Genesis to Revelation through the lens of being in God's "image."* I will attempt
to walk us through the Bible's teaching on what it means to be part of God's
family. Typically, projects that study the people of God throughout the Bible
do so in light of the biblical covenants, whereas my goal here is to sketch the
nature of the covenant community in possessing the divine image. God uses
the covenants in preserving and restoring his image in humanity.

A secondary purpose in writing this project is to lay the foundation for
several of the volumes in the Essential Studies in Biblical Theology (ESBT).
This series, as described in the series preface, outlines the major themes of
the Bible from Genesis to Revelation. My project will explore issues that are
taken up and developed in several of the individual ESBT volumes, such as
temple, king, priest, prophet, creation, and redemption. I will endeavor to
show how these salient themes are organically related to one another.

Chapter One

THE CREATION OF ADAM

IT WAS WEDNESDAY, December 2, 2009, and I was teaching Greek 101 to a group of undergrad students at Wheaton College. My phone rang. While I typically do not keep my phone on while I teach, this time was different. My wife was nine months pregnant with our first, and she was ready to pop. "I think it's happening!" she exclaimed. I darted off, picked her up, and drove to the hospital in record time. Fast-forward twelve hours, and it was game time. My wife and I had taken a Lamaze class together and had heard countless stories from our friends, but nothing prepared us for the real thing. It was three in the morning, and I was about to meet Judah Benjamin for the first time.

His hair was dark brown, and his baby skin was tan. He had his mother's dark brown eyes, but there was no doubt about it—he was my son. Growing up, we look *up* to our parents to determine our resemblances. But when we have children, we look *down*. For the first time in my life, someone was in my "image" and "likeness" at some level.

For us to understand what it means to be part of the people of God, we must begin with the creation of Adam and Eve in the divine image. This project begins with the creation of the cosmos and humanity's role within it. The task before us in this chapter is straightforward: sketch the nature of Adam and Eve's being created in the divine image and how the first couple relates to God and the world around them. What does it mean that Adam and Eve are in God's likeness, and what are his expectations for them? As we will discover below, humanity is fashioned to dwell in God's presence and tasked with the responsibility to bring his glory to the ends of the earth.

THE COSMOS AS GOD'S TEMPLE

A careful reading of Genesis 1–2 reveals God creating a vast cosmic temple, wherein he dwells and sovereignly rules. Parallels between the creation account in Genesis 1–2 and the construction of the tabernacle in the book of Exodus are many, and several scholars argue that God is indeed fashioning a cosmic temple in Genesis 1–2.[1] Elsewhere in the Old Testament, the cosmos is compared to Israel's temple:

> He built his sanctuary like the heights,
>> like the earth that he established forever. (Psalm 78:69;
>>> cf. 1 Chronicles 28:2; Isaiah 66:1-2)

Moshe Weinfeld, for example, astutely juxtaposes God creating the cosmos and Moses establishing the tabernacle, as shown in table 1.1.[2]

The parallels between these two accounts are difficult to ignore, especially when we consider them in light of the Pentateuch's unity. Exodus is meant to be read in light of Genesis 1–3.

Even the layout of Israel's temple symbolically depicts the order of the cosmos. The outer courtyard of the temple contained the washbasin and the altar, symbolizing the sea and the land (1 Kings 7:23-25; Ezekiel 43:14-16). Moving a step closer to God's presence, the second section of the temple, or the holy place, symbolized the visible heavens and was lined with gold, containing the altar of incense (1 Kings 6:20), the bread of the Presence resting

---

[1]J. Richard Middleton, *The Liberating Image: The Imago Dei in Genesis 1* (Grand Rapids: Brazos, 2005), 81-82.

[2]Moshe Weinfeld, "Sabbath, Temple and the Enthronement of the Lord: The Problem of the *Sitz im Leben* of Genesis 1:1–2:3," in *Mélanges biblique et orientaux en l'honneur de M. Henrie Cazelles*, ed. André Caquot and Matthias Delcor, AOAT 212 (Kevelaer, Germany: Butzon & Berker, 1981), 501-12.

GENESIS 1–2	EXODUS 39–40
"God saw *all that he had made*, and it was very good." (Genesis 1:31)	"Moses inspected *the work* and saw *that they had done it* just as the LORD had commanded." (Exodus 39:43)
"Thus the heavens and the earth *were completed* in *all* their vast array." (Genesis 2:1)	"So *all* the work on the tabernacle, the tent of meeting, *was completed*." (Exodus 39:32)
"By the seventh day God *had finished the work he had been doing*." (Genesis 2:2)	"And so Moses *finished the work*." (Exodus 40:33)
"Then God *blessed* the seventh day." (Genesis 2:3)	"So Moses *blessed* them." (Exodus 39:43)
"Then God . . . *made it holy*." (Genesis 2:3)	"Anoint the tabernacle and everything in it; *consecrate it* and all its furnishings." (Exodus 40:9)

Table 1.1

on a table (1 Kings 7:48), and ten lampstands fashioned out of gold (1 Kings 7:49). The final and most sacred section of the temple was the holy of holies, which symbolized the invisible heavens, where God dwells. This partition, separated by an embroidered curtain, was also lined with gold and housed the ark of the covenant. Above the ark, two cherubim faced one another, symbolizing the throne of God in heaven, which is also surrounded by cherubim (Psalm 80:1; 99:1; cf. Isaiah 6). In summary, the connections between the cosmos and Israel's temple are overwhelming. Michael Morales rightly concludes, "The cosmos was understood as a large temple and the temple as a small cosmos."[3]

Israel's tabernacle and temple are just models of something greater—the entire cosmos. The earthly temple corresponds to something greater—the cosmic temple over which God rules. As an illustration, my kids and I enjoy playing with Legos, and one of our favorite sets is the Millennium Falcon. This thousand-piece set includes all sorts of details that are found in the *Star Wars* films, even a detailed hyperdrive system! Not for a second, though, do my kids and I believe that the Lego set is the real Millennium Falcon. It's just a model.

[3]L. Michael Morales, *Who Shall Ascend the Mountain of the Lord? A Biblical Theology of the Book of Leviticus*, NSBT 37 (Downers Grove, IL: InterVarsity Press, 2015), 40.

Another important detail found in Genesis 1 is the creation of lights. On day one, God creates light (Genesis 1:3), whereas on day four God fills the heavens with lights: "And God said, 'Let there be *lights* in the vault of the sky to separate the day from the night'" (Genesis 1:14). The word "lights" here in the creation narrative is noteworthy, as the same term is applied to the lampstand in Israel's tabernacle: "the lampstand that is for *light* with its accessories, lamps and oil for *the light*" (Exodus 35:14; cf. Exodus 39:37; Numbers 4:9). The lampstand in the tabernacle and Israel's temple illuminated the holy place, symbolizing God's presence among his people. The lights strewn about the cosmos function as cultic luminaries that burn brightly throughout God's cosmic temple. In this vein, the seven lights affixed to the lampstand in Israel's temple probably symbolized the seven lights of the visible sky (sun, moon, and five planets).[4] These lights "mark sacred times, and days and years" (Genesis 1:14). Creation follows a fixed calendar that calls to mind God's purpose in creating all things. That is, the lights set the rhythm of the created order, so that all of creation may be oriented toward God and reminded to worship him.[5]

When God finished creating the cosmos, he rested from the creative process, but this resting is unlike our modern conception of rest. I often associate resting with watching football with my kids on Sunday afternoons, but resting in the Old Testament is quite different. God resting after six days entails his climactic enthronement as King over the cosmos (Genesis 2:2; cf. 2 Chronicles 6:41; Isaiah 66:1). Perhaps an illustration would help here. One of my favorite hobbies is woodworking on the weekends. I enjoy working with wood—measuring (twice!), cutting, sanding, and finishing. Some time ago, I built a table for our dining room. To use the language of Genesis 1, in six days I created the table, and on the seventh day, I "rested," when I moved the table inside my house and dined on it. God resting on the Sabbath occurs when he executes his sovereign rule over his creation.

So why did God graciously construct a cosmic temple? Why does the creation of the cosmos parallel the construction of the tabernacle? Simply

---

[4]Vern Poythress, *The Shadow of Christ in the Law of Moses* (Brentwood, TN: Wolgemuth & Hyatt, 1991), 18-19.
[5]Morales, *Who Shall Ascend*, 45.

put, God built a cosmic house to occupy. Much like an individual constructing a large estate on a plot of land, where the owner desires to move in and manage the property, God desires to rule the created order and fill it with his resplendent presence. Quite simply, the universe is designed to house the veritable glory of God.

EDEN AS A TEMPLE

An additional detail we glean from Genesis 1–2 is the depiction of Eden as a sanctuary resting on a mountain. Though God dwells in all his fullness in the invisible heavens, his presence has partially descended in the Garden of Eden. Just as Israel's temple comprises three tiers, so also does the earth.

Eden is the center of God's activity on the earth, where God dwells and gives Adam and Eve his law and instructs them how they are to honor him. Much like Sinai, Eden ought to be understood as a mountain that houses God's glory. Genesis 2:10-14 adds several seemingly odd details about the flow of water: *"A river watering the garden flowed from Eden*; from there it was separated into four headwaters. The name of the first is the Pishon. . . . The name of the second river is the Gihon. . . . The name of the third river is the Tigris. . . . And the fourth river is the Euphrates."*

Living in the South, we deal with severe storms and heavy rains on a regular basis. Without fail, water pools at the bottom of my front yard, and I suddenly find myself owning waterfront property! Water only flows in a downward direction. So one aspect of these seemingly incidental details about flowing water in Genesis 2:10-14 is that Eden is situated on a mountain. Mountains in the Old Testament and the ancient world are often associated with the presence of a deity (e.g., Isaiah 2:2; 65:9; Micah 4:1-4).

In Genesis 3:8, the bit about God's "walking" in the garden is akin to God's walking in Israel's midst in Leviticus 26:12, a clear reference to the tabernacle (cf. Deuteronomy 23:14). The prophet Ezekiel even calls Eden "the garden of God . . . the holy mount of God" (Ezekiel 28:13-14). Two trees stand in the middle of the garden—the tree of life and the tree of the knowledge of good and evil (Genesis 2:9). Partaking of the tree of life appears to have sustained Adam and Eve's existence. Meanwhile, the tree of the knowledge of good and evil may have been the place of judgment where Adam and Eve were to act on behalf of God and judge all unclean things, casting them out of the garden.[6]

The point is clear enough. Adam and Eve enjoyed God's presence in Eden. The closer the couple remained toward the center of the created order, the nearer they were to God and his life-giving presence. God's glory is at the center of the created order. His glory sustains and nourishes all living things. This insight about Eden being the holy of holies on the earth demonstrates two important points: God ultimately wants to dwell with the created order in all his fullness, and Adam and Eve will play a critical role in accomplishing that goal.

THE CREATION OF THE DIVINE IMAGE

After God creates his cosmic temple, he begins to enter into it, rule over it, and dwell with humanity. On day six, at the pinnacle of creation, he creates Adam and Eve to rule on his behalf. God's full presence remains in the invisible heaven, yet his partial presence comes down to Eden to dwell with Adam and Eve. This is similar to God's fully dwelling in heaven yet residing in the holy of holies of the temple.

When God creates Adam and Eve in his image, they are to become his official representatives on earth. According to Genesis 1:26, God intends to create humanity in his image "so that they may rule over the fish in the sea and the birds in the sky, over the livestock and all the wild animals, and over all the creatures that move along the ground." One verse later, God fulfills his intention, and humanity is created in God's own image (Genesis 1:27).

Extensive research in the last several decades on ancient creation accounts and a continued interest in ancient Near Eastern archaeology have sharpened our understanding of "image" here in Genesis. It was common in the ancient Near East for a deity to be functionally represented by an idol or an image. For example, one Egyptian text reads,

Well tended is *mankind*—god's cattle,
He made sky and earth for their sake,

---

[6]G. K. Beale, *A New Testament Biblical Theology: The Unfolding of the Old Testament in the New* (Grand Rapids: Baker Academic, 2011), 35.

> He subdued the water monster,
> He made breath for their noses to live.
> They are *his images*, who came from his body,
> He shines in the sky for their sake;
> He made for them plants and cattle,
> Fowl and fish to feed them.[7]

The combination of "mankind," "sky and earth," "images," "plants and cattle," and "fowl and fish" resonates with Genesis 1:26-27. Another text explicitly connects "image" with ruling:

> Hear what I did, exceeding the ancestors,
> I the *King, image of god*,
> Living *likeness* of Atum!
> Who left the womb marked as *ruler*,
> Feared by those greater than he!
> His father knew, his mother perceived:
> He would be *ruler* from the egg,
> The good god, beloved of gods,
> The *Son of Re*, who acts with his arms,
> Piye beloved-of-Amun.[8]

This passage is an introduction to the Nubian king's conquests in the Upper and Lower portions of Egypt. The entire proclamation, inscribed on a stela, is a testimony to the king's conquests in the land. Like the previous passage, this one also uses similar language to Genesis 1:26-27. Here kingship is linked to "image," "likeness," and "son." These two passages are just a sample of a plethora of ancient texts that resonate with the creation account in Genesis 1–2.

The creation of Adam and Eve in Genesis 1 is the climax of the created order. God waits to create the first couple until day six. In the first three days, God creates realms (Genesis 1:3-13), and then he fills up each realm in days four to six with his creatures (Genesis 1:14-31). Each realm is governed by a particular ruler. The heavens (day one) are governed by lights (day four);

---

[7]"Merikare," trans. Miriam Lichtheim (*COS* 1.1.35.66).
[8]"The Victory of Stela of King Piye (Piankhy)," trans. Miriam Lichtheim (*COS* 2.2.7.42).

the waters above and below (day two) are governed by sea creatures and birds (day five); the land (day three) is governed by animals (day six). Remarkably, when God creates Adam and Eve, they are designed to "*rule* over the fish *in the sea* and the birds *in the sky* and over every living creature that moves *on the ground*" (Genesis 1:28). Humanity is therefore created to rule over the rulers of two of the three realms.

Just as God rules over the entire cosmos, so humanity, created in the image of God, was to rule over the earth and its inhabitants. Ruling over the earth is not intended for a few, but for an entire community. All of humanity is to rule.[9] *Fundamentally, being created in God's image means that Adam and Eve represent him on the earth in all their thoughts and actions. It is the divine imprint of God in humanity that reflects his divine attributes and functions in the threefold office of king, priest, and prophet.*

The first human was imbued with certain qualities that God alone possesses. These qualities are both internal, or ontological, and external, or functional. God possesses certain qualities or attributes that he passes along to Adam—love, peace, justice, ability to rule, and so on. Adam is not God, nor does he perfectly mirror God in every way (Adam was not omnipresent). The line between Creator and creature is quite clear. As God's image, Adam represents God on earth and is created to remain submissive to and wholly dependent on God.

ADAM AND EVE AS KINGS

Theologians often explain the divine image in three categories: king, priest, and prophet. These three long-held classifications are helpful on many levels, so I will adopt them going forward. The first couple were created as kings, priests, and prophets, and though these offices overlap with one another, each of them possesses distinct traits and goals. The first office that we will explore is the office of kingship. It is perhaps the most dominant office in Genesis 1–2. Adam and Eve were created as vice regents over the created order. Simply stated, vice regents rule on behalf of others; they do not rule independent of the supreme ruler. In Genesis 1–2, Adam and Eve are to remain utterly dependent on God and extend his rule on the earth.

---

[9]Hans Walter Wolff, *Anthropology of the Old Testament*, trans. Margaret Kohl (Philadelphia: Fortress, 1974), 161.

I noted above how imaging God is tethered to ruling on behalf of him over the created realm. Genesis 1:28 explicitly commands Adam and Eve to "subdue" and "rule over" creation. God fashioned them for a specific purpose, and they are required to fulfill it. In Genesis 2:7 Adam receives the "breath of life." In the first creation account, Adam is created in the image and likeness of God, whereas in the second account Adam receives the "breath of life." According to the narrative, therefore, receiving the breath of life is perhaps parallel in some way to being created in the image of God; particularly, being created from the "dust" may be likened to kingship.[10]

Later in Genesis 2, we discover one of Adam's first accomplishments as king: "Now the LORD God had formed out of the ground all the wild animals and all the birds in the sky. He brought them to the man to see what he would name them; and *whatever the man called each living creature, that was its name. So the man gave names to all the livestock, the birds in the sky and all the wild animals*" (Genesis 2:19-20). As God sovereignly named the various facets of the cosmos (Genesis 1:5, 8, 10), so too Adam executes his rule by naming the animals. In doing so, the first man is discerning patterns within the created world and assigning function. Adam is beginning to achieve what he was designed to do. So far, so good.

Even King David looks back on Genesis 1–3 and underscores Adam's position to rule:

When I consider your heavens,
    the work of your fingers,
the moon and the stars,
    which you have set in place,
what is mankind that you are mindful of them,
    human beings that you care for them?
You have made them a little lower than the angels
    and *crowned them with glory and honor.*
You made them *rulers over the works of your hands*;
    you put *everything under their feet.* (Psalm 8:3-6)

---

[10]Walter Brueggemann, "From Dust to Kingship," *ZAW* 84 (1972): 1-18.

In sum, Adam and Eve were created for the purpose of extending God's rule over the created order, so that his divine presence would radiate out from them. God rules over the cosmos in the invisible heavens with the angels, and the first couple is charged with appropriating that rule on earth. It may not be far-fetched to suggest that Eden was the "throne room" of Adam and Eve's kingdom.[11]

We are now in a position to ask why. Why are Adam and Eve commanded to rule over the earth? Was not the created order deemed "good" (Genesis 1:10, 18, 25)? Reading between the lines a bit, we can see that some aspects of the created order require "subduing" and portions of it remain incomplete. God is not simply being rhetorical or hyperbolic when he commissions Adam and Eve in Genesis 1:28. Recall that the earth, like Israel's temple, contains three gradations of holiness. Eden is the holy of holies, the garden is the holy place, and the outer world is the outer court. So, perhaps, as there are gradations of holiness, we can surmise that there are gradations of God's rule extending throughout the earth.

According to Genesis 1:28, Adam and Eve are to establish a community of faithful children who systematically appropriate God's rule to the farthest corners of the earth. God's people are to engage every aspect of the created world and bring it into conformity with God's character and rule. The farthest region, the outer world, could be considered chaotic at some level (though not sinful). Just as God brings order out of chaos in Genesis 1, Adam is responsible for bringing order out of chaos. Any hint of nonconformity must be immediately addressed. As we will see in the following chapter, Adam and Eve, upon encountering the serpent in Eden (the holy of holies!), should have immediately judged it and expelled it from God's presence. Casting out the serpent is one concrete way in which the first couple was to exercise their office of kingship.

Consider an illustration. I do a fair amount of DIY projects on my house and cars. Whenever something breaks, my first impulse is to look for a YouTube clip on how to fix the issue. A while ago, I installed a sprinkler system in my front yard, which probably was not the best project to undertake in the blazing hot month of July in Mississippi. My grass needed water to survive

---

[11]Stephen G. Dempster, *Dominion and Dynasty: A Theology of the Hebrew Bible*, NSBT 15 (Downers Grove, IL: IVP Academic, 2003), 62.

in the summer, and I grew tired of spending precious time moving the sprinkler around the yard. It took me a week or so, but I eventually got it up and running. In a small, small way, by installing a sprinkler system in my yard, I was like Adam in taking control of my environment. My environment needed attention, and it was my job to take care of it. As Adam and Eve begin to have a family, and animals begin to multiply, the first couple is expected to exercise control of Eden and the surrounding territory.

ADAM AND EVE AS PRIESTS

Adam and Eve are not only created to extend God's rule, they are also fashioned to mediate God's presence and to worship and serve before him. As priests, Adam and Eve are to minister in God's garden sanctuary in Eden and expand God's glory to the ends of the earth. Recall that Eden is the holy of holies, and the garden is the holy place. In the Old Testament, only priests are able to minister before the Lord, and only the high priest can enter into the holy of holies (Leviticus 16). Adam and Eve serve and worship the Lord on the mountain of Eden and intimately commune with him.

According to Genesis 2:15, God "took the man and put him in the Garden of Eden *to work it* [ʿbd] *and take care of* [šmr] *it.*" As many commentators point out,[12] these two verbs, "work" and "watch over," are found elsewhere in the Old Testament referring to priests ministering in the temple: "They [the Levites] *shall guard* [šmr] all the furnishings of the tent of meeting, and *keep guard* [šmr] over the people of Israel as they *minister* [ʿbd] *at* the tabernacle" (Numbers 3:8 ESV; cf. Numbers 8:26; 18:7). In Genesis 1, God creates Adam and Eve in his image so that they may rule, subdue, and fill the earth (Genesis 1:28). Here in Genesis 2, we begin to see how the divine commission is worked out in some detail. Genesis 2:15 unpacks the general commission of Genesis 1:28. In a word, Adam will accomplish God's command to rule and fill the earth (Genesis 1:28), at least in part, *by* working and watching over the garden (Genesis 2:15).

Priests in the Old Testament have a number of important duties. Critical to their ministry is to take "care of the sanctuary and the altar" (Numbers 18:5).

---

[12]E.g., Gordon J. Wenham, *Genesis 1–15*, WBC 1 (Waco, TX: Word, 1987), 67.

For example, on a daily basis, the priests burned incense (Exodus 30:7-9) and tended the seven lamps on the golden lampstand (Exodus 27:21). Each week the twelve loaves of bread were prepared and placed on a golden table (Leviticus 24:5-9). The priests were even responsible for teaching the Israelites the Torah (Deuteronomy 31:9-13; 33:10) and what was considered clean and unclean. They were also charged with maintaining the purity of the temple and God's people and were to guard against all uncleanness that threatened to defile the sanctuary. By offering up various sacrifices, the priests purified the sacred space and the Israelites (Leviticus 22; Numbers 28–29). Sin had to be dealt with before the worshiper could enjoy fellowship with the Lord. Like the removal of dirt and grime from a window, one purpose of the temple rituals was to remove sinful contaminants that defiled the worshiper. A holy God can only dwell in a holy temple among a holy people.

God's holy character is magnificently on display in the layout of Israel's camp during their wilderness journeys. At the center of the camp is the tabernacle, the place where God dwells. The entire structure, including the courtyard, holy place, and holy of holies is deemed holy. But even within the holy tabernacle, only the back room is considered the most holy. Moving outside the courtyard of the tabernacle, Israel's camp is considered "clean," and everything outside the camp is "unclean." So, there are three levels of gradation: holy, clean, and unclean. Determining what is unclean is tricky when we examine Israel's purity laws. On one level, uncleanness can refer to immoral activities, such as murder and theft, or to behavior tied to idolatry, such as drinking blood (see Leviticus 17–20). On the other, uncleanness can refer to anything that lacks perfection or is incomplete, such as skin diseases or the loss of bodily fluids (see Leviticus 11–15). In the latter case the moral component isn't necessarily in view. The point of uncleanness in both scenarios is critical: God accepts only that which is pure, perfect, and ordered. But the issue of holiness is one notch above cleanness. Holiness is married to God's glory. In a word, "*To be clean means to be fit for the Presence of God, while to be holy means that one belongs to God.*"[13]

So, God entrusts the priests with the responsibility to discern between what is holy, clean, and unclean. According to Leviticus 10:10, priests were

---

[13]Morales, *Who Shall Ascend*, 155 (emphasis original).

to "distinguish between the holy and the common, between the unclean and the clean." The priests were charged with applying God's truth to the created order, as they decided what violated the divine law and what did not. Remarkably, the word for "distinguish" here in Leviticus 10:10 is also found in Genesis 1:4, 7, where God "separated" light from the darkness and "separated" the water under the vault from the water above it. God is here making distinctions in the creation of the world. So, the priests carry out the same creative task when they "separate" clean from unclean.[14] Since the priests are created in God's image, they share a similar function to God on the earth. As God separated the light from the dark in the creation of the cosmos, the priests separate the unholy from the holy on the earth. They do what God did.

If we keep in mind some of these insights about Israel's priests, then Adam and Eve's priestly responsibilities come into focus. Adam and Eve minister before the Lord in Eden, the holy of holies. Since Eden is the holiest part of the created order, and everything inside it is considered "most holy," then it's likely that Adam was to study Eden's environment—the trees, the animals, and so on, and learn what is deemed holy and acceptable to God. Recall that the tree of the knowledge of good and evil is planted in Eden (Genesis 2:9). Adam must learn how to execute judgment wisely.

As Adam and Eve descended the mountain, the environment may have become less holy. Here in the second gradation of holiness, or the holy place, Adam was probably responsible to pay attention to those things in the environment that were unable to remain in God's presence. This location surrounding the mountain includes less holy things. Finally, the least holy territory is the outer world. Here in the "outer courts" lies all that is unfit for God's holy presence in Eden. While still considered holy, the uninhabitable region contains items that lack absolute perfection and completion. The farther Adam and Eve journeyed from Eden, the farther they traveled away from God's presence. The environment gradually became less and less holy (see fig. 1.1).

---

[14]Rodney K. Duke, "Priests, Priesthood, " in *Dictionary of the Old Testament: Pentateuch*, ed. T. Desmond Alexander and David W. Baker (Downers Grove, IL: IVP Academic, 2003), 651.

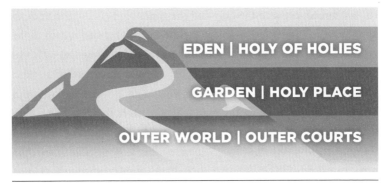

Figure 1.1

Though the entire created order is considered good and holy, creation still remains incomplete, for God's presence is restricted to Eden. Genesis 2:15 states, "God took the man and put him in the Garden of Eden to work it and take care of it." As the first horticulturist, Adam is here charged with transplanting Eden and extending it beyond the mountain. He is, quite simply, commissioned to expand God's presence. As Eden expands, so does God's glory. We don't know how this would have worked precisely, as the text doesn't say, but we can at least be confident that Eden was to encompass the entire earth. This would require a considerable amount of effort as Adam would need to study the environment and learn how he could transplant Eden. There wasn't a local Home Depot selling Edenic sod! This is where Genesis 1:28 comes to the fore: "God blessed them and said to them, '*Be fruitful* and *increase* in number; *fill* the earth.'" Adam and Eve are to bear godly children who fill the earth with God's presence. Adam and Eve would not accomplish this task alone. They are commanded to raise up offspring that will join with them in obeying the divine commission. The ultimate intention of humanity is, therefore, for the whole earth to be filled with God's "images" that radiate his glory.

ADAM AND EVE AS PROPHETS

The third and final office of Adam and Eve is the prophetic role. A prophet is an individual who hears God's voice and speaks on behalf of God to his people. The prophet is, simply put, the embodiment of God's truth. Prophets in the Old Testament were commissioned by God and his angels, often referred to as the divine council (see 1 Kings 22:19-22; Job 1:6-12; Isaiah 6:8; Zechariah 3:1-4). The prophetic word is the very word of God on earth. Not more, not less. As Israel's history unfolded, the prophetic role became more complex and integral. The early prophets, such as Moses and Deborah, assisted with Israel's military operations and the general execution of justice. But when Israel gained a king, the prophets became advisors to the king (e.g., Nathan, Elijah, Elisha). When Israel began spiraling into idolatry and rebellion, the prophets began speaking directly to the nation (e.g., Isaiah, Jeremiah).

Though Adam and Eve's prophetic role is not as prominent as their kingly and priestly roles, Genesis 1–2 contains a few clues that the first couple indeed functioned as God's mouthpiece. The commission of Genesis 1:28 requires that Adam and Eve serve as prophets: "God blessed them and said to them, 'Be fruitful and increase in number; fill the earth.'" In order to obey this command, they are required to bear children and instruct them in the ways of the Lord. But before the parents teach their children, they must understand God's law. In Genesis 2:16-17 God issues his law to Adam: "You are free to eat from any tree in the garden; but you must not eat from the tree of the knowledge of good and evil, for when you eat from it you will certainly die." Together with the divine commission of Genesis 1:28, Adam must take this prohibition to heart, meditate on it, and relate it to his wife. As Adam's family grows, his prophetic role will inevitably increase, since more teaching will be required.

The first man is responsible to learn how the Genesis 1:28 commission concretely relates to all of life; Adam must learn how to increase the territory of Eden. He is then required to teach his insights to his wife and children, and then the children must repeat the process. The expectation is that God's people will be godly and continually teach his precepts to one another. All of humanity is expected to embody the truth. Adam and Eve's prophetic role in Genesis 1–2 therefore manifests itself in two ways: exemplifying God's law and communicating it to others.

CONCLUSION AND APPLICATION

Genesis 1–2 narrates God's creating the heavens and earth to be his cosmic sanctuary, where he dwells and sovereignly rules. Every square inch of creation is designed to house the full glory of God. At the pinnacle of his creative activity, God fashions Adam and Eve in his image to rule as kings on his behalf, to serve and mediate his glory as priests, and to embody and teach God's law to one another as prophets. All the while humanity is to remain wholly dependent on God and represent him faithfully on the earth.

Despite God's intimate communion with the first couple in the Garden of Eden, his full presence dwells in the invisible heaven with the angels. Even before the fall, God and humanity remained separated—God in heaven and Adam and Eve on the earth. By creating a cosmic temple, God reveals that he intends on dwelling with humanity in all his fullness. Even at the beginning of the story, Genesis 1–2 looks forward to the very end of history, when heaven and earth will be joined together. Though perfectly created, the cosmic temple remains incomplete. Sin can infest the original creation. The cosmos and humanity, then, must be altered to house all of the glory of God. God's aim is for humanity to spread this glorious presence over the entire earth, so that it may be transformed into the new heaven and earth. Once the earth is permanently transformed, God's full presence will descend with great finality and will dwell with humanity and creation for eternity.

The marriage between Adam and Eve in Genesis 2:21-25 is the climax of the narrative thus far. This union is incredibly important for the spread of God's glory. It is the means by which it will be accomplished. This marriage is also the template for every subsequent Israelite union (see, e.g., Malachi 2:15; Matthew 19:5; Ephesians 5:31) and the pattern for Yahweh's relationship with his people. The marriage between Adam and Eve, a male and a female, is unquestionably held out as a model for the proper union. This explains why we get the wording: "That is why a man leaves *his father and mother* and is united to his wife, and they become one flesh" (Genesis 2:24). Adam and Eve didn't have a father and a mother! We live in a culture that is hostile to the biblical definition of marriage, but Christians must not be vague or acquiesce.

If Adam and Eve obey God's commission in Genesis 1:28 and his law in Genesis 2:16-17 by producing godly descendants, expanding the boundaries of Eden, and filling the earth with God's glory, keeping his commands and subduing evil, then the earth will be transformed into an incorruptible creation, evil will be abolished, and humanity will inherit incorruptible bodies.

God will descend to earth to rule and dwell with humanity for all of eternity. But if humanity fails to obey, then they will "certainly die" (Genesis 2:17). Theologians refer to this *conditional* agreement as the "covenant of works." Upon perfect obedience, blessing is assured, but death and estrangement from God await Adam and Eve if they disobey.

What does it mean to be a human, to be in God's image? It means that we were originally designed to image God on earth. D. A. Carson puts it this way:

> The least that "image of God" language suggests, in addition to human personhood, is that human beings are not simply hairless apes with cranial capacities slightly larger than those of other primates, but that we are accorded an astonishing dignity; that human beings are moral creatures with special privileges and responsibilities; that there is implanted within us a profound capacity for knowing God intimately . . . that we have a hunger for creating things—not, of course, *ex nihilo*, but in art, building, expression, thought, joy of discovery, science, technology; that we have a capacity for personal relations with other persons.[15]

God put an indelible mark on the first couple to rule on his behalf, mediate on and enjoy his presence, and live in accordance with his law, reminding one another of his truths. To be anything less is to be unhuman.

RECOMMENDED READING

Beale, G. K. *The Temple and the Church's Mission: A Biblical Theology of the Dwelling Place of God.* NSBT 17. Downers Grove, IL: IVP Academic, 2004.

Dempster, Stephen G. *Dominion and Dynasty: A Theology of the Hebrew Bible.* NSBT 15. Downers Grove, IL: IVP Academic, 2003.

Hoekema, Anthony A. *Created in God's Image.* Grand Rapids: Eerdmans, 1986.

Middleton, J. Richard. *The Liberating Image: The Imago Dei in Genesis 1.* Grand Rapids: Brazos, 2005.

---

[15]D. A. Carson, *Gagging of God: Christianity Confronts Pluralism* (Grand Rapids: Zondervan, 1996), 205.

Chapter Two

FALL AND RESTORATION

GENESIS 1–2 DESCRIBES the creation of the cosmos as a temple and Adam and Eve as fashioned to be kings, priests, and prophets dwelling in this cosmic temple. They are to produce a kingdom of godly descendants, rule over the created order, embody and mediate God's law to one another, and fill the earth with the presence of God. But as we turn to Genesis 3, the first couple fails on all fronts. That didn't take long. The narrative does not reveal the length of time between Genesis 2 and Genesis 3, but one gets the impression that not much time has transpired. This chapter will attempt to articulate both how the fall affected the first couple and how God's goal for creation remains intact despite their disobedience. Humanity is unable to fulfill their end of the bargain, so God will do it for them.

THE FALL

Following Adam and Eve's marriage in Genesis 2:21-25, the narrative immediately turns to the serpent's deception of Eve. The serpent is introduced as being "more crafty than any of the wild animals the LORD God had made" (Genesis 3:1). We learn here that the serpent is part of the created world, the same world over which Adam and Eve were to exercise dominion. By associating the serpent with creation, the implication is that Adam and Eve were tasked with ruling over the serpent.

The temptation threatens all three offices of Adam and Eve, striking at the heart of being created in God's image. As God's images, the first couple represents him on the earth and serves on his behalf. But the serpent allures them to cast off God's image and become independent of God and function at his level. The temptation, at its heart, is to become like God—to rule and to think like God.

It appears that the serpent tempts Eve while she and Adam are in Eden, the mountain of God and the first sanctuary. Notice that the serpent first tempts Eve and strategically bypasses Adam. According to the narrative, Adam is created first (Genesis 2:7, 20-22) and appears responsible for leading, teaching, and representing his family (cf. Genesis 2:22; 2 Corinthians 11:3; 1 Timothy 2:13). In Genesis 3:9 God approaches Adam and not Eve to give accountability for their actions. Adam is thus the representative head of all humanity. By approaching Eve, the serpent is attempting to dismantle the family structures God originally set in place. Adam, who appears to be within earshot (Genesis 3:6), should have immediately intervened.

As kings representing God on earth, Adam and Eve should have quickly subdued the serpent, a ghastly unclean animal (see Leviticus 11; Deuteronomy 14).[1] They should have prevented the serpent from slithering into Eden in the first place! If we read between the lines, it is possible to conclude that the first couple had let their guard down and were not proactively warding off unclean animals. Jeffrey Niehaus keenly observes, "The presence of the foe [in the garden] presents the human with an opportunity to wage war."[2]

As priests, Adam and Eve should have rid the sanctuary of Eden from defilement. The serpent embodies evil and rebellion. Simply put, it is the greatest expression of uncleanness. We noticed in chapter 1 that God's glory is tied to three gradations: holy, clean, and unclean. The serpent is categorized two notches down from holiness, and mixing the unclean with the holy is abhorrent to God. The first priests should have recognized the unclean creature and eradicated it from God's temple.

---

[1]Gordon J. Wenham, *Genesis 1–15*, WBC 1 (Waco, TX: Word, 1987), 73.
[2]Jeffrey J. Niehaus, *Biblical Theology*, vol. 1, *The Common Grace Covenants* (Wooster, OH: Weaver, 2014), 103.

As prophets, Adam and Eve should have been meditating on God's law (Genesis 2:16-17). The exchange between the serpent and Eve focuses on the specifics of that law. God was quite clear: "You must not eat from the tree of the knowledge of good and evil, for when you eat from it you will certainly die" (Genesis 2:17). When the serpent tempts Eve, notice how he tweaks the command: "Did God really say, 'You must not eat from any tree in the garden'?" (Genesis 3:1). No, he did not say that. Adam and Eve are indeed "free to eat from any tree in the garden" (Genesis 2:16), just not the tree of the knowledge of good and evil.

Notice how when Eve responds to the initial temptation, she fails to repeat God's law correctly: "The woman said to the serpent, 'We may eat fruit from the trees in the garden, but God did say, "You must not eat fruit from the tree that is in the middle of the garden, and *you must not touch it*, or you will die"'" (Genesis 3:2-3). God didn't say anything about not touching the fruit. God also said that they would "certainly die" (Genesis 2:17), whereas Eve softens the curse when she claims that she would simply "die" (Genesis 3:3). The fall reveals that the couple failed to live up to their identity as "images." God designed them to rule, to worship, and to embody God's law, yet they failed to keep the "covenant of works" in all three respects.

Adam and Eve's refusal to follow God's commands stemmed from their fundamental belief that their way was better. When God's word is ignored, sin is inevitable. As much as I enjoy designing and building furniture from scratch, I detest purchasing stock furniture from a store and putting it together. I would rather do everything myself. When I open the box and pull out each piece of particle board, I begin to assemble each piece. The problem, though, is that I obtusely refuse to read the directions. I do not like to be told how to put something together and in what order. Inevitably, I manage to put some part on backward or upside down. I want to do things my way. In our eyes, our way is always better.

THE EFFECTS OF THE FALL

Immediately after partaking of the fruit, Adam and Eve "realized they were naked" (Genesis 3:7). The word here for "naked" is related to the Hebrew word for "crafty" (Exodus 21:14; Joshua 9:4; Job 5:13). A few verses earlier, in

Genesis 3:1, the serpent was described as "more *crafty* than any of the wild animals." The point is that, as a result of the fall, the couple is beginning to take on characteristics of the serpent.[3] Instead of representing God on the earth, Adam and Eve are now beginning to represent the serpent.

This insight brings us to an important principle that will be highlighted throughout this book: images will always be transformed into their object of worship. G. K. Beale rightly states, "What people revere, they resemble, either for ruin or restoration."[4] Images are meant to reflect and refract God,[5] so if Adam and Eve obey God, they become more like him. Their divine image was to become more and more aligned with God's character. But because they believed and trusted in the serpent instead of God, they began to transform into the serpent's image. Instead of manifesting the traits of God on earth, they and their descendants would manifest the traits of the serpent. In the following verses, Adam and Eve shift the blame and are unwilling to answer the Lord truthfully (Genesis 3:11-13). They, like the serpent, are attempting to deceive.

The more that we worship and adore Christ, the more we will be transformed into his image. This is what sanctification entails—the process of becoming like Christ. Praying often, reading God's Word, and enjoying sweet fellowship with believers are some concrete ways in which we become more sanctified. One way in which we can determine whether we are ridding ourselves of idolatry is to take an inventory of our thoughts and ambitions. Do we spend most of our week satisfied in Christ, or are we consumed with ourselves? Are our thoughts and affections inward or are they outward toward Christ?

God then outlines the curses that he will execute because of their disobedience. When God curses Eve, the divine commission of Genesis 1:28 hangs in the background:

> I will make your pains in childbearing very severe;
>   with painful labor you will give birth to children. (Genesis 3:16)

---

[3]Meredith G. Kline, *Genesis: A New Commentary*, ed. Jonathan G. Kline (Peabody, MA: Hendrickson, 2016), 22.

[4]G. K. Beale, *We Become What We Worship* (Downers Grove, IL: IVP Academic, 2008), 16.

[5]J. Richard Middleton, *A New Heaven and a New Earth: Reclaiming Biblical Eschatology* (Grand Rapids: Baker Academic, 2014), 49.

The point is that Eve's fulfillment of the commission will be incredibly difficult. Adam and Eve will indeed populate the earth, but it will come at a high cost. In addition, the second part of the curse reads,

> Your desire will be for your husband,
>   and he will rule over you. (Genesis 3:16)

The language is difficult here, but the verse appears to say that discord will emerge within the marriage relationship. The fall did not destroy Eve's identity as queen, but it did affect how she will rule. Instead of ruling the created world together with her husband and preserving the internal structure of marriage, Eve will attempt to "rule" over her husband and wrest control from him.[6]

In Genesis 2:15 God commanded Adam, the first priest, to "work" and "take care" of Eden. That command echoes throughout Adam's curse:

> Cursed is the *ground* because of you;
>   through *painful toil* you will eat food from it
>   all the days of your life.
> It will produce thorns and thistles for you,
>   and you will eat the plants of the field.
> By the sweat of your brow
>   you will eat your food
> until you return to the ground,
>   since from it you were taken;
> for dust you are
>   and to dust you will return. (Genesis 3:17-19)

Adam will continue to operate as a priest, but he will do so under great peril (see Genesis 3:23). The curse climaxes in Adam's death. The ultimate price of attempting to be "like God" is alienation from him.

Each and every day we are reminded of our fallen condition. Though believers enjoy a restored image in Christ, indwelling sin remains. All thoughts

---

[6]Victor P. Hamilton argues, "It [3:16b] means a desire to break the relationship of equality and turn it into a relationship of servitude and domination. The sinful husband will try to be a tyrant over his wife. Far from being a reign of co-equals over the remainder of God's creation, the relationship now becomes a fierce dispute, with each party trying to rule the other" (*The Book of Genesis: Chapters 1–17*, NICOT [Grand Rapids: Eerdmans, 1990], 202).

and actions are still tainted with sin, and the penalty for sin is for God to pour out his wrath on us and for us to be completely estranged from him. But in Christ, God's wrath has been appeased and we have drawn near to God's presence. Christians would do well to remember on a daily basis the justification and right standing before God that we enjoy in Christ. We would also do well to contemplate our previous condition outside of Christ. Recognizing the gravity of our sin leads to a deeper appreciation of God's grace in Christ.

THE PROMISE OF REDEMPTION

Embedded within the serpent's curse is a profound promise of redemption. Genesis 3:15 states that God "will put enmity" between the serpent and his ungodly offspring and the godly descendants of Adam and Eve. Here we have a war of "seeds," the basic outline that will permeate the remainder of the Bible's story:

> And I will put enmity
> Between you and the woman,
> And between *your seed and her seed*;
> He shall bruise you on the head,
> And you shall bruise him on the heel. (Genesis 3:15 NASB)

The fate of the godly and the ungodly are intertwined. The godly are those who enjoy a restored image, whereas the ungodly are those who have a perverted image or an "anti-image." The term *anti-image*, used throughout this project, refers to an individual who is hostile to God and is the opposite of those who enjoy a restored image. The anti-image still retains all three offices of being in the image of God, yet it uses the offices for its own selfish ambition. Here the term *anti-image* is an apt description of the serpent's seed. The two lines will wage war with one another, culminating in the decisive defeat of evil: "He [a righteous descendant of Eve] shall bruise you [the serpent] on the head." Redemption is guaranteed. A godly king, who is in the pristine, perfect image of God, will vanquish the serpent, the embodiment of the anti-image, at the very end of history. All those who trust in this redeemer will inherit his victory.

This king will accomplish what Adam and Eve failed to accomplish. They failed to rule over the serpent and rid Eden of it, so now a faithful descendant will arise and obey where they disobeyed. Some theologians refer to this promise as the "covenant of grace" because God himself will ensure the success of a future king and the preservation of a godly community. This is an *unconditional* covenant or agreement. It is not dependent on human effort, as God himself will ensure its fulfillment.

Immediately following Adam's curse, Genesis 3:20 states that "Adam *named his wife Eve*, because she would become the mother of all the living." Recall that Adam demonstrated his royal office by naming the animals in Genesis 2:20. He named the animals in a way similar to God's naming of the cosmos (Genesis 1:5, 8, 10). So, despite the fall, Adam appears to trust in God's promise in Genesis 3:15 and once again demonstrates his identity as a king. Adam recognizes that Eve will play a pivotal role in the process of redemption.

In Genesis 3:15 God promises that the serpent will be defeated and that the divine commission of Genesis 1:28 will be accomplished. In Genesis 3:21 God begins to make good on that promise: "The LORD God made garments of skin for Adam and his wife and clothed them." In the Old Testament garments are often associated with inheritance. As Gordon Hugenberger points out, there is "an association between the donning of clothes and the acquisition of throne rights (or inheritance rights)."[7] This may explain Adam and Eve's meager attempt to regain their loss of inheritance and kingly position by making a garment of fig leaves (Genesis 3:7). If so, then they were attempting to restore their inheritance and relationship with God on their own terms. But according to the Genesis account, these garments manufactured from fig leaves were unfit, so God made acceptable garments (Genesis 3:21). God began the process of restoring Adam's image so that he could rule, worship, and obey. Only God possesses the power to redeem.

A key dimension of the gospel is that God satisfied his own demands in his Son's work. We are simply unable to pull ourselves up by our own moral bootstraps. If we live apart from Christ, we are attempting to dress ourselves with fig leaves. Instead, we must trust in God, who works on our behalf and clothes us with the perfect righteousness of the last Adam.

---

[7]Gordon Hugenberger, *Marriage as a Covenant: Biblical Law and Ethics as Developed from Malachi*, VTSup 52 (Leiden: Brill, 1994; repr. Grand Rapids: Baker, 1998), 199n130.

LIFE IN EXILE

Though God begins to restore Adam and Eve's image and the first couple once again enjoys harmony with God, damage has been done. The fall severely affected the first couple and the created order. Sin dwells within and affects every aspect of their image, both functionally and ontologically. Humanity and creation now rebel against the Creator. Because of Adam and Eve's corrupted image and proclivity to assert independence from God (Genesis 3:22), the Lord expels them from Eden. Adam and Eve were to expel the serpent from the garden, but because they disobeyed, they ironically are now expelled. Adam and Eve are unclean!

Genesis 3:24 reads, "After he [God] drove the man out, he placed *on the east side* of the Garden of Eden cherubim and a flaming sword flashing back and forth to guard the way to the tree of life." They are now kings without a kingdom, priests without a temple, and prophets without the intimate voice of God. The book of Genesis casually references the eastward direction on a number of occasions (Genesis 4:16; 13:11; 25:6), underscoring humanity's movement away from Eden, away from God's glory. If we are fully human when we dwell in God's presence, then the further we wander from that presence, the less human we become. Humans are created to dwell in the glory of the Lord. But as the narrative of the Pentateuch unfolds, the solution is for Eden to go with humanity.

UNGODLY IMAGES

From Genesis 4 to Revelation 20, the Bible narrates great hostility between those whose images are beginning to be restored and those whose images begin to collapse from within. Genesis 4–5 is paradigmatic for how the godly line and the ungodly line begin to interact with one another and fulfill the promise of Genesis 3:15. Genesis 4 opens with the birth of two children. Abel "kept flocks," whereas Cain "worked the soil" (Genesis 4:2). Recall that Adam was responsible for both of these tasks (Genesis 2:15, 19-20), so we can surmise that Adam's descendants are attempting to carry on the Genesis 1:28 commission. God may have rejected Cain's priestly offering because it was taken from a "cursed" soil (Genesis 3:17).[8] Cain, like his parents, is confronted with

---

[8]Gary A. Herion, "Why God Rejected Cain's Offering: The Obvious Answer," in *Fortunate the Eyes that See: Essays in Honor of David Noel Freedman*, ed. Astrid B. Beck, Andrew H. Bartelt, Paul R. Raabe, and Chris A. Franke (Grand Rapids: Eerdmans, 1995), 52-69.

two options: obey God and offer up an animal sacrifice from Abel's lot (Genesis 4:4) or become wise in his own eyes and disobey God. The Lord tells Cain to function as a king, as he was created to do, and "rule over" sin (Genesis 4:7). Instead, sin eventually rules over him, and Cain murders his brother. We begin to see the image of God collapsing on itself, as Cain uses his royal identity for his own gain. "Murder is perhaps the ultimate usurpation of authority, because death is God's judgment on fallen humans, and its timing should belong to him alone."[9] Sin rules over Cain, and Cain wrongly rules over his godly brother Abel (cf. Genesis 9:6).

God approaches Cain, much liked he approached Cain's parents in the garden, and asks him, "Where is your brother Abel?" (Genesis 4:9). Instead of speaking truthfully as a prophet should, Cain responds, "I don't know. . . . Am I my brother's keeper?" (Genesis 4:9). Up to this point, Cain has failed in all three offices: he offered up the wrong sacrifice (priest), ruled over his brother (king), and lied to God (prophet). As a result, Cain is sentenced to a life away from God in the "land of Nod, east of Eden" (Genesis 4:16). Adam is exiled from Eden, but Cain is farther still. He finds himself as a "restless wanderer," estranged from the Lord (Genesis 4:12). Once again, exile from God's glory is the penalty for disobedience. The story of Cain is the story of Adam and Eve.

The narrative then goes on to describe how Cain lives outside of God's presence. According to Genesis 4:17, Cain built a city and then "named it after his son Enoch." Building a city is a natural development of being in God's image. God, according to Genesis 1–2, constructs a cosmic temple, so it's not surprising that those in his image do the same. But Cain perverts his God-given responsibility as a priest and instead of building a city that brings glory to God's name, he builds a city for the glory of his son Enoch. The habits of the anti-image are beginning to take root.

The next few verses reveal how the image of God in Cain's line continues to develop in fascinating ways: "Adah gave birth to Jabal; he was the father of those who live in tents and *raise livestock*. His brother's name was Jubal; he was the father of all who *play stringed instruments and pipes*. Zillah also

---

[9]Niehaus, *Common Grace Covenants*, 134.

had a son . . . who forged *all kinds of tools out of bronze and iron*" (Genesis 4:20-22). Humanity is beginning to understand and interact with the created order in new and exciting ways. Here we see the development of farming, music, and manufacturing processes. Genesis 1:28 and Genesis 2:15 somehow linger in the background of these verses. Despite the fall, humanity still possesses God's image. We are created to understand and engage the world around us. Yet, Lamech's wickedness in Genesis 4:23-24 demonstrates that fallen humanity will always contort and pervert the divine calling. Daniel Migliore puts his finger on this tension when he writes, "We human beings are a mystery to ourselves. We are rational and irrational, civilized and savage, capable of deep friendship and murderous hostility, free and in bondage, the pinnacle of creation and its greatest danger."[10]

GODLY IMAGES

With the ungodly line climaxing in Lamech's wicked behavior, humanity's outlook appears bleak. How will the divine commission of Genesis 1:28 be accomplished? Where will the promised redeemer of Genesis 3:15 come from? The answer lies at the end of Genesis 4: "Adam made love to his wife again, and she gave birth to a son and named him Seth, saying, 'God has granted me another child in place of Abel'" (Genesis 4:25). As we find out later, the godly line will continue through the line of Seth. The restored image of God will be preserved through Seth and his descendants. The chapter ends with a stunning contrast: "At that time people began to call on the name of the LORD" (Genesis 4:26). Cain built a city and "named it after his son Enoch" (Genesis 4:17), whereas the godly seed preserved in the line of Seth brings honor to "the name of the LORD." Cain's perverted image brings honor to himself and his descendants, but the restored image in Seth and his family glorifies the Lord. The hallmark of a restored image is whether one's actions honor the name of the Lord.

At the beginning of Genesis 5, we learn *how* the restored image is passed down. This passage is critical in how we understand the nature of restoration—how a person's rebellious image transforms into a restored image (see table 2.1).

---

[10]Daniel L. Migliore, *Faith Seeking Understanding: An Introduction to Christian Theology*, 2nd ed. (Grand Rapids: Eerdmans, 2004), 139. Quoted in Graham A. Cole, *God the Peacemaker*, NSBT 25 (Downers Grove, IL: IVP Academic, 2009), 53.

GEN 1:26-28A NASB	GEN 5:1-2 NASB
Then God said, "Let Us make man in Our image, according to *Our likeness*"; . . . *God created man* in his own image, in the image of God *he created him;* male and female he created them. God blessed them.	This is the book of the generations of Adam. In the day when *God created man*, He made him in the *likeness of God.* He *created them male and female,* and *he blessed them* and named them Man in the day when *they were created.*

Table 2.1

The rehearsing of the creation account at this point in the narrative is telling. This is the second genealogy thus far. Genesis 4:17-26 comprises the first, but, unlike that genealogical section, this one is prefaced with a review of Genesis 1:26-28. Perhaps Genesis 5 is viewed, according to the narrative, as the beginning of the fulfillment or the continuation of the Genesis 1:26-28 mandate and blessing. Genesis 5:3 literally reads: "he begot in his likeness, according to his image." Some translations unfortunately miss the emphasis. The thrust of Genesis 5:3 is not necessarily Adam becoming a father but the impartation of his image to Seth. As Victor Hamilton suggests, Adam is doing to Seth what God has done to him: "The reference to Gen. 1 at the start of this chapter [Genesis 5] permits a contrast between a divine creative act and human creative acts. In a sense, Adam and his posterity are doing what God did."[11] Just as God imparted his image to Adam, so also Adam imparts his image to Seth. Genesis 5 is indeed intended to be read in light of Genesis 1:26-28 as a continuation or fulfillment, implying that Adam's descendants have begun to rule and subdue the earth.

By passing on his image to Seth, Adam is obeying God's commands in Genesis 1:28: "Be fruitful and increase in number; fill the earth and subdue it." Adam and Eve are beginning to execute their offices of king, priest, and prophet. Though the text is silent on this, we should probably assume that the first couple faithfully taught God's law to Seth and tangibly demonstrated how to rule over the created order, worship the Lord, and embody God's commandments. Certainly, the godly line is still affected by sin in that they do not perfectly obey the Lord in every facet of their lives; nevertheless, they are living in light of their restored image, and their actions flow from their redemption.

[11]Hamilton, *Book of Genesis*, 255.

I have two boys, Judah and Simon, and parenting, as I have learned through the years, is incredibly difficult. I wish I could give my kids instructions once and expect that they will follow through without any issues. But parenting requires constant attention and prodding. My wife and I come alongside our kids and teach them about life, God's Word, and the world around them. Every aspect of life flows from being created in the divine image, and parents must explain to their kids what this looks like concretely. Parents are responsible for instructing their children about what it means to be in God's image and how to represent him faithfully on the earth.

CONCLUSION AND APPLICATION

As a result of the fall, the nature of being in God's image became self-destructive. The fall didn't efface the divine image, but it did pervert it. The kingly, priestly, and prophetic aspects of God's image are now tools for destruction. Humanity was created to bring glory to God, but now humanity will attempt to bring glory to itself. This is idolatry of the highest sort—the worship and adulation of one's self. The ungodly line, as anti-kings, will rule viciously by abusing one another and the created order. These descendants, as anti-priests, will also defile the created order and worship everything but the one true God. The ungodly line, as anti-prophets, will deceive and embody all teaching that is hostile to God.

Genesis 1-5 is an emotional rollercoaster. God creates the world to be his cosmic house and fashions Adam and Eve to manage and represent him on the earth. But right out of the gate the story takes a turn for the worse. Sin infected the created order and cast it into a state of rebellion. What about God's original plan? How can rebellious humanity obey the divine commission of Genesis 1:28? The answer: God graciously and sovereignly overcomes Adam and Eve's sin and restores their image. Though the godly line still has indwelling sin, God will now go with them and ensure that his expectations are met.

The line of Cain, though wicked, reveals an important aspect of being human. Despite possessing a perverted and selfish image, Cain and his descendants begin to develop in new and creative ways (Genesis 4:17-22). We find here the origin of music and the arts and the building blocks of technology. Humanity is putting their divine image to work. Jerram Barrs captures the creative component of being in the image of God when he claims,

Our work in any field of the arts will be imitative. We will be thinking God's thoughts after him—painting with his colors; speaking with his gift of language; exploring and expressing his sounds and harmonies; working with his creation in all its glory, diversity, and in-built inventiveness. In addition, we will find ourselves longing to make known the beauty of life as it once was in Paradise, the tragedy of its present marring, and the hope of our final redemption.[12]

One of the blessings of the internet is our awareness of one another's talents and gifts. I am in constant awe of my friends. They build houses, play the piano, paint murals, snap jaw-dropping photographs, write remarkable books, and on and on. Though we are all fashioned in God's image and each of us is a king, priest, and prophet, we express those realities with incredible variety. Since God is inexhaustible in his being, no two people are exactly alike. At one level, each person is fundamentally the same; that is, we all bear the same image. Yet on another level, we are all different. We express God's character in innumerable ways on a daily basis. I enjoy working with my hands as I build furniture and work around the house. My meager ability to build reflects on a small scale God's ability to build on a cosmic scale. The same could be said for my wife, who plays the piano. Her ability to play notes on a page flows from God's rejoicing in himself. Every human is created in God's image and possesses gifts and talents that reflect God's infinite creative might.

RECOMMENDED READING

Block, Daniel I. *For the Glory of God: Recovering a Biblical Theology of Worship.* Grand Rapids: Baker Academic, 2014.

Hoekema, Anthony A. *Created in God's Image.* Grand Rapids: Eerdmans, 1986.

Lints, Richard. *Identity and Idolatry: The Image of God and Its Inversion.* NSBT 36. Downers Grove, IL: IVP Academic, 2015.

Munson, Paul, and Joshua Farris Drake. *Art and Music: A Student's Guide.* Wheaton, IL: Crossway, 2014.

Peterson, Ryan S. *The Imago Dei as Human Identity: A Theological Interpretation.* JTISup 14. Winona Lake, IN: Eisenbrauns, 2016.

---

[12]Jerram Barrs, *Echoes of Eden: Reflections on Christianity, Literature, and the Arts* (Wheaton, IL: Crossway, 2013), 26.

Chapter Three

ISRAEL'S CREATION AND FALL

DESPITE THE FALL, the goal of Genesis 1–2 remains intact—God dwelling intimately with his restored people in the new creation. His commission to Adam and Eve to fill the earth with godly offspring is never shelved. This same commission is passed to Noah: "Be fruitful and increase in number; multiply on the earth and increase upon it" (Genesis 9:7). Noah, a second Adam figure, is responsible to form a community of godly kings, priests, and prophets. But like Adam, Noah fails (Genesis 9:20-27). The commission is then picked up and applied to Abraham, but when Abraham receives the commission, we discern a shift. The original commission is retained while couched in a series of incredible promises:

> "I am God Almighty; *walk before me faithfully and be blameless.* Then I will make my covenant between me and you and *will greatly increase your numbers."*
>
> Abram fell facedown, and God said to him, "As for me, this is my covenant with you: *You will be the father of many nations.* . . . *I will make you very fruitful; I will make nations of you, and kings will come from you. I will establish my covenant as an everlasting covenant between me and you and your descendants after you for the generations to come.* . . . The whole land of Canaan, where you

now reside as a foreigner, *I will give as an everlasting possession to you* and your descendants after you; and I will be their God."

Then God said to Abraham, "As for you, *you must keep my covenant, you and your descendants* after you for the generations to come." (Genesis 17:1-9; cf. Genesis 12:1-3)

The imperatives to "walk . . . faithfully" and "keep my covenant" are met with the promises of "greatly increasing" Abraham's descendants and of his becoming "very fruitful" in the land of Canaan. The reason why these commands interlock with divine promises is because humanity is still responsible to carry out the original commission to fill the earth with God's glory. But because of the fall, humanity is unable to accomplish this task alone. God graciously promises Abraham and his descendants that he will meet his own original demands *through* them. The Abrahamic covenant, a concrete manifestation of the covenant of grace (Genesis 3:15), ensures that the original command is satisfied.

As the book of Genesis marches forward, Adam's commission is reaffirmed and steadily yet incompletely fulfilled at nearly every major turn in the narrative (Genesis 26:3-4, 24; 28:3-4, 13-14; 35:11-12; 48:3, 15-16). At the beginning of Exodus, Israel finds herself not in the land of Canaan but in Egypt. Nevertheless, according to Exodus 1:7, the people of Israel were "exceedingly *fruitful*; they *multiplied* greatly, increased in numbers and became so numerous that the land was *filled* with them." Genesis 1:28 is indeed taking root, yet the earth is far from being completely filled with God's glory.

This chapter attempts to explain how the nation of Israel broadly fits into God's plan to redeem humanity and dwell with them in the new heavens and earth. How is Israel, a corporate Adam, expected to rule as kings, mediate God's presence, and embody his law? What difference does the temple make? How does God's presence among his people energize them to fulfill the original commission?

THE CREATION OF ISRAEL AND THE DIVINE IMAGE

God graciously preserved the godly line through the descendants of Seth, culminating in the person of Noah (Genesis 3:15; 5:29). The narrative of Genesis portrays Noah, fashioned in God's image, as representing a new humanity and fulfilling the offices of king, priest, and prophet (Genesis 6–9).

Mount Ararat, too, is reminiscent of Eden (Genesis 8:1-5). God promises Noah that his descendants, through the line of Shem, will enjoy God's presence (Genesis 10–11). The call of Abraham signals a new phase in God's program in that the fulfillment of the divine commission of Genesis 1:28 is now gathering considerable steam. What began with a pair of individuals in Eden will now continue on in an entire nation in the Promised Land. The narrative of Genesis is the story of God's graciously restoring and preserving his people.

Exodus opens with Jacob's offspring (the "seventy") signifying new beginnings, a new humanity in Egypt (Exodus 1:5). The promised struggle of Genesis 3:15, between the two images or seeds, runs throughout the whole of Genesis and especially here in the early chapters of Exodus. As Exodus unfolds, we quickly learn how Pharaoh and Egypt embody the anti-image, whereas Moses and Israel represent the restored image. As the anti-image, Pharaoh attempts to rule over Israel, the firstborn of God (Exodus 4:22), by oppressing the Israelites through hard labor. So God will in turn rule over the firstborn of Egypt (Exodus 11:1-10). God brings his people out of the clutches of Egypt, through the waters of redemption, to Mount Sinai. Israel is formed out of the chaos of Egypt and planted in Eden, the base of Mount Sinai.

God is fulfilling his promises to Adam and Eve (Genesis 3:15) and to Abraham (Genesis 12:1-3; 15:1-21; 17:3-22). He promised that Abraham's descendants would be a mighty nation, and God is making good on those promises! Many argue that Israel's experience at Sinai parallels the creation account of Adam and Eve. William Dumbrell juxtaposes Adam and Israel in the manner shown in table 3.1.[1]

ADAM AND EVE	ISRAEL
Created outside Eden	Created outside Canaan
Created to function as kings and priests	Created to function as kings and priests
Condition to stay in Eden through law	Condition to stay in Canaan through Torah
Exiled from Eden	Exiled from Canaan

Table 3.1

---

[1]William Dumbrell, "Genesis 2:1-17: A Foreshadowing of the New Creation," in *Biblical Theology: Retrospect and Prospect*, ed. Scott J. Hafemann (Downers Grove, IL: InterVarsity Press, 2002), 61-62.

At Sinai God creates a corporate Adam, a magnificent people group that is responsible for ruling as kings, worshiping as priests, and embodying God's law as prophets. Isaiah 43:1 reflects back on God's creating Israel using the identical wording found in Genesis 1–2:

> But now, this is what the Lord says—
>> he who *created* you, Jacob,
>> he who *formed* you, Israel.

Just as God created Adam and Eve and installed them in Eden, so too he creates Israel and installs them in the Promised Land (see fig. 3.1).

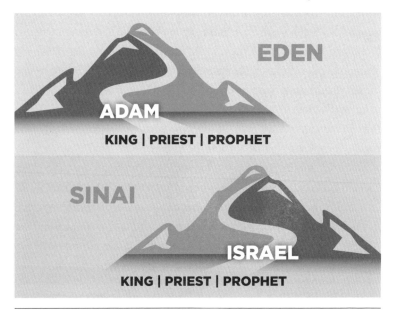

Figure 3.1

The nation of Israel is fashioned as a corporate image. Deuteronomy 4:20 may very well have this in mind. It reads, "But as for you, the Lord took you and brought you *out of the iron-smelting furnace*, out of Egypt, to be the people of his inheritance." In contrast to humans manufacturing false images (Deuteronomy 4:15-19), God manufactures Israel in his pristine image in the "iron-smelting furnace" of Egypt. Often in the Bible, the people of God function as a single unit. For example, the apostle Paul depicts the church, a community composed of individuals, as a "body" (e.g., 1 Corinthians 12:12-27; Ephesians 4:15-16, 25; 5:23; Colossians 1:18). The community of redeemed saints, despite its incredible diversity, functions as a single entity in light of its union with Christ. The same could be said for the people of Israel gathered at Sinai, who are collectively deemed the "firstborn son" of God (Exodus 4:22) and a corporate Adam.

Viewing the church as the collective body of Christ has tremendous application to our daily lives. If we grasp the significance of being in solidarity with one another, we realize the gravity of our behavior. Sin not only affects us in a personal manner but also radiates out within the body of Christ. Sin harms our hearts and the hearts of those around us. On the flip side, righteous living reinforces the solidarity we enjoy within the church.

SINAI AS A TEMPLE

Mount Sinai is a focal point of much of the Pentateuch. The first half of Exodus narrates Israel's dramatic arrival to the mountain (Exodus 1:1–18:27), while the remainder of Exodus (19:1–40:38), the entire book of Leviticus, and roughly the first third of Numbers (1:1–10:10) take place at Sinai. The nation of Israel would camp at Sinai for nearly eleven months. It is here where God would graciously promise to Israel that he would be their God and that they would be his people.

In the last few decades, several scholars have begun to draw parallels between Mount Sinai and Israel's tabernacle and temple. Like Eden and the tabernacle, Sinai is a "mountain of God" (Exodus 3:1) having three gradations of holiness (see fig. 3.2).[2]

At the base, the least holy area, Moses encounters the burning bush, where he is commanded to remove his sandals because he is standing on "holy ground" (Exodus 3:5). Later in the narrative, the nation of Israel will also gather at the base of the mountain as they await their leader to meet with God (Exodus 19:2-24). Like the priests ministering in the holy place, the second tier of holiness is restricted to only Moses, Aaron, Nadab, Abihu, and the seventy elders of Israel (Exodus 24:1). The highest point of Sinai is

---

[2]Illustration found in Angel Manuel Rodríguez, "Sanctuary Theology in the Book of Exodus" *AUSS* 24 (1986): 133.

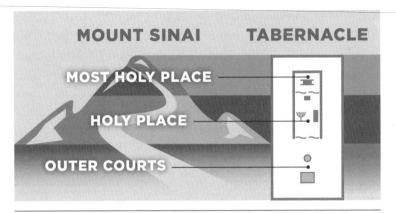

Figure 3.2

reserved for Moses alone, much like only the high priest is permitted to enter into the holy of holies.

What's the significance of Sinai as a temple? How does it inform our understanding of being in God's image? The temple of Sinai, if we can call it that, is the theological framework for understanding the creation of Israel. Israel's release from Egyptian captivity and march through the Red Sea symbolizes the nation of Israel's redemption and new life. The result of their redemption is to worship the Lord at Sinai, the dwelling place of God. Israel is redeemed *so that* the nation may worship and enjoy God's presence at the mountain (e.g., Exodus 3:12, 18; 5:3; 7:16; 8:1). And like Adam and Eve, God creates Israel as an image—a corporate one—designed to reflect and refract his character on the earth. Image and God's glory go hand in hand.

We will now explore the ways in which Israel as a nation is created to be kings, priests, and prophets. Once again, we need to keep in mind that these three offices overlap with one another, so it can be difficult at times to parse them neatly into three distinct strands.

Israel as kings. God is now going to form the seed of Abraham as a corporate Adam, a nation, to go into another garden, the Promised Land. If they can be loyal to the word of the Lord in that garden, subdue and rule over the earth, and convert the nations, then the new heavens and earth would arrive, God's consummate rule would begin, and he would dwell fully with his people. "Israel, the family of Abraham, is God's true humanity. Her land is God's land. Her enemies are God's enemies, and they will be subject to her in the same way that the beasts were subject to Adam."[3]

Israel is to function corporately as a king on a few levels. Like Adam and Eve were to judge all forms of wickedness at the tree of the knowledge of good and evil in the garden (Genesis 2:9), the nation is responsible for evaluating and judging all forms of sin in the Promised Land. They are expected to filter all their actions and those of the surrounding cultures through God's law and determine whether any thought or intention is not in accordance with it. Adam and Eve were to bring order to the uninhabitable regions that were far from the mountain of Eden. But they failed to subdue the serpent and resist temptation. So now God raises up the nation of Israel to bring order to the chaos of Canaan. As kings, Israel is to bring everything under subjection to the reign of God.

Another area in which the Israelites are to work out their kingly status is the eradication of the Canaanites. God promised to Abraham, Isaac, and Jacob that their descendants would inherit a land (Genesis 13:14-17; 15:16-21; 17:8; 35:11-12; 50:24). God and Israel are to dwell together—where he will be their God and they will be his people. For Israel to live in the land of Canaan, though, they first need to conquer the wicked Canaanites. The Promised Land was, as Deuteronomy 7 explains, infested with idolatry. Since God is to dwell with Israel in the Promised Land, all forms of idolatry and rebellion must be expelled.

Central to conquering the Canaanites is *how* Israel was to rule and subdue their enemies. Recall that Adam and Eve were created in God's image as vice regents who ruled on behalf of God. Like the first couple, the nation of Israel is to appropriate God's rule to the land of Canaan. If Israel adheres to the covenant, God fights for them (Exodus 23:20-33). A most prominent depiction of God in the Old Testament is his identity as Israel's divine warrior (e.g., Psalm 18:7-15; 24:7-10; 68:4; 104:1-3). If Israel obeys God's decrees, God will fight on behalf of the nation (Joshua 11:6-9). If Israel disobeys, though, God promises to fight against them (1 Samuel 4:1-11; Lamentations 2:4-5).

It is tempting for us to take matters into our own hands rather than unswervingly trust God. Instead of walking by faith (2 Corinthians 5:7), our

---

[3]N. T. Wright, *The Climax of the Covenant: Christ and the Law in Pauline Theology* (Minneapolis: Fortress, 1993), 23.

natural pattern of behavior is to walk by sight and attempt to govern our own lives. The Bible tells us time and again that only God is sovereign and all-knowing and that we should trust him in every situation.

Israel as priests. Exodus 19:5-6 states that *if* Israel perfectly obeys God's law, then the nation would be a "kingdom of priests." The result of obedience is service to the nations. As priests mediate God's presence to the Israelites, so too the nation Israel is to mediate God's presence to the surrounding nations. Israel must be, as John Durham notes, "committed to the extension throughout the world of the ministry of Yahweh's presence."[4]

I mentioned in chapter one how Adam and Eve were created in God's image to be priests in the sanctuary of Eden. Fundamentally, a priest was responsible for taking care of the temple, discerning what was clean and unclean, and mediating God's presence to others. Priests, simply put, were charged with ensuring that humanity is prepared to worship the one true God.

According to Genesis 1:28, God's original design is that the entire earth be filled with his glory and populated with godly individuals that reflect and refract his character. The fall, of course, made fulfilling this command impossible without divine intervention. So God promised to Abraham that he would be a father of a mighty nation that would become a beacon of light to the surrounding nations (Genesis 12:1-3; 15:1-21; 17:1-22). God will fulfill Genesis 1:28 through the covenant with Abraham. Now, with Israel encamped at Sinai, God's original intention will continue through the covenant at Sinai. If Israel perfectly obeys the covenant, the nation will fulfill the commission of Genesis 1:28.

God's glory is to shine forth in a dark world. I remember on one occasion the power going out in my house due to a strong storm, leaving me feeling utterly helpless. I didn't know what was in front of me or behind me. I was terrified. I fumbled around until I found a flashlight. Though small, the light illuminated the room, and I was once again able to make out the pieces of furniture and what lay ahead. Likewise, the image of God imprinted on the nation of Israel was to be a beacon of light in a land ensconced in darkness.

In addition to mediating God's glory, another dimension of Israel's priestly service is their commitment to preserving the sanctity of the temple and the

---

[4]John Durham, *Exodus*, WBC 3 (Waco, TX: Word, 1987), 263.

Promised Land. It may not be a stretch to conceive of the Promised Land as a gigantic temple, at least in some sense, wherein God dwells with Israel. In fact, Exodus 15:15-17 makes this connection:

> The people of Canaan will melt away. . . .
> You will bring them [Israel] in and plant them
>   on the mountain of your inheritance—
> the place, LORD, you made for your dwelling,
>   the sanctuary, Lord, your hands established.

God is holy, and he can only dwell in the midst of a holy people in a holy land. Recall that Adam and Eve were to minister before the Lord in Eden, the holy of holies (Genesis 2:15). The farther Adam and Eve journeyed from Eden, the farther they traveled away from God's presence, and the environment gradually became less and less holy. The first priestly couple was responsible for removing all unorderly things from the garden, so that God's presence could remain with them. But, by allowing the unclean serpent to slither into Eden, Adam and Eve failed to live up to their priestly office.

At Sinai, God creates a corporate Adam and charges them to be holy and set apart from the nations, so that he can dwell in their midst (Exodus 19–31). Israel is to be not only clean but also holy—the highest and most acceptable position before God. Within the nation of Israel, God ordained a distinct office of priests (Exodus 28–29), and the priests represent the people to God as they minister in the tabernacle. And as Israel settles in the Promised Land, the nation must immediately expel all forms of spiritual uncleanness.

Israel as prophets. The final dimension of the nation of Israel functioning as the corporate image of God is their prophetic office. A prophet receives the word of the Lord and is his mouthpiece on the earth, embodying truth. Adam and Eve were to learn God's decrees, meditate on them, and proclaim them to their descendants. At Sinai, God gives Israel his law, and the nation commits to keeping the covenant. According to Exodus 24:7, Moses reads the Book of the Covenant to the people and they, in response, proclaim, "We will do everything the LORD has said; we will obey." Here the Israelites swear that they will learn and adhere to the law of God. They promise that

they will embody God's word and promote it within their communities in
the Promised Land.

God summarizes the entire law in the Ten Commandments (Exodus 20:1-17).
The first four commandments relate to God's relationship with his people, and
the last six concern the Israelites' relationship to one another. Fundamental
to the Ten Commandments are the prohibitions in the first and second commandments to "have no other gods" and to "not make for yourself an image"
(Exodus 20:3-4). God alone creates images; images cannot create other images.
Since Israel is in the image of God, they are forbidden to fashion any images
that resemble God or anything else. The only permitted images are humans,
since they, when restored, accurately display the wonder and character of God.

Central to the prophetic office of Israel is the preservation of the first and
second commandments. By far, Israel's greatest struggle is idolatry, and a
cursory glance throughout her history yields a considerable amount of material dedicated to Israel's failure in this regard. Prophet after prophet pleads
with Israel and her kings to resist the temptation to worship other gods. For
example, at the end of 2 Kings, God discloses *why* he sent Israel into Babylonian exile: "I am going to bring disaster on this place and its people . . .
because they have forsaken me and burned incense to other gods and aroused
my anger *by all the idols their hands have made*" (2 Kings 22:16-17).

THE FALL OF ISRAEL

Like the first couple, Israel must form a godly community that obeys God's
law, rules over the entire created realm, and mediates God's presence. God
covenants with them by obligating himself to grant life to those who perfectly
obey (Leviticus 26:1-13; cf. Deuteronomy 28:1-14) and death to those who do
not (Leviticus 26:14-46; cf. Deuteronomy 28:15-68). Resembling their parents
in the garden, the Israelites immediately break God's law by committing
idolatry through worshiping the golden calf (Exodus 32; cf. Hosea 6:7). This
is, as one commentator states, "Genesis 3 all over again."[5] On the surface
Aaron forged a golden calf, and Israel explicitly broke the first and second
commandments (Exodus 20:3-4). But the breach of the second commandment

---

[5]Terence E. Fretheim, *Exodus*, IBC (Louisville: John Knox, 1991), 279.

revealed a more fundamental issue in the hearts of the Israelites—a lack of trust in God's word. God promised that he would dwell with his people and that his life-giving presence would nourish and protect them (Exodus 19:5-6). But they failed to believe him, so they took matters into their own hands. As with Adam and Eve in the garden, God's word was insufficient. The Israelites wanted to dictate the terms of their preservation. They wanted to be in charge of their destiny. They wanted to be gods.

Exodus 32:1-4 narrates the Israelites' growing restless in waiting for Moses to descend the mountain. They convince Aaron to fashion a golden calf. Instead of worshiping the Lord, the Israelites worship an idolatrous calf. The narrative then graphically describes the Israelites as rebellious cattle. Israel is a "stiff-necked people" who were "running wild" and "out of control" (Exodus 32:9, 25). God transforms Israel into the very thing she worships—the golden calf.[6] Recall that Adam and Eve were beginning to transform into the image of the serpent in an attempt to deceive God in Genesis 3:10-13. Instead of worshiping the Lord and becoming more and more like him, the Israelites worship the calf and become calf-like in their behavior. Like Adam, Aaron refuses to take responsibility for his actions and blames the people for manufacturing the calf (Exodus 32:24).[7]

The Israelites failed as kings to believe that God would rule over their enemies. They asked Aaron to manufacture a god "who will go before" them and protect them (Exodus 32:1). They failed as priests because they worshiped an idolatrous image. And they failed as prophets because they failed to preserve and protect the first two commandments. The result of Israel's idolatry is, like Adam and Eve's fall, catastrophic, as three thousand Israelites are killed at the hands of their own people (Exodus 32:27-29). Despite Moses' attempt to make atonement for Israel's sin, God promises to "punish them for their sin" (Exodus 32:31-34). "Like Adam, Israel is put into a sacred space to exercise a kingly/priestly role (cf. Ex 19:4-6) . . . like Adam, Israel is given laws by which the divine space

---

[6]G. K. Beale, *We Become What We Worship* (Downers Grove, IL: IVP Academic, 2008), 76-86.
[7]Victor P. Hamilton, *Handbook on the Pentateuch*, 2nd ed. (Grand Rapids: Baker Academic, 2005), 222.

is to be retained. Finally, Israel, like Adam, transgresses the law and so too is expelled from the divine space."[8]

As the book of Numbers unfolds, we learn that except for Caleb and Joshua, the entire first generation of Israelites would never enter the Promised Land (see fig. 3.3).

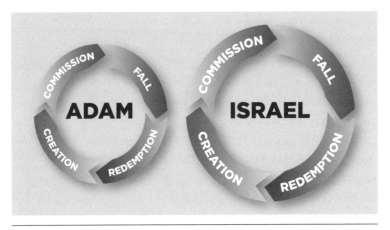

Figure 3.3

The effects of Israel's fall continue on in their story. King Saul's rule is marked not by service to Israel but my selfish intentions. His ministry quickly spirals out of control, paving the way for David to arrive on the scene. Despite King David's promising start, he commits adultery with Bathsheba, leading to the murder of Uriah. David's own son Absalom even conspires against him. The height of Israel's kingship arrives with King Solomon. Resembling Adam, Solomon expands Israel's borders, builds the temple, and ushers in a time of unparalleled peace within Israel. Yet, fissures in the foundation of Solomon's reign begin to surface. Idolatry and division within the monarchy soon ensue. Instead of obeying God's laws, keeping the covenant, and ruling on behalf of God as Adam should have done in the garden, Israel's kings in the north and the south brazenly commit idolatry and rule selfishly. During the period of the divided monarchy righteous kings are few and far between.

---

[8]William J. Dumbrell, "Genesis 2:1-17: A Foreshadowing of the New Creation," in *Biblical Theology: Retrospect and Prospect*, ed. Scott J. Hafemann (Downers Grove, IL: InterVarsity Press, 2002), 62.

John Calvin famously stated that "man's nature, so to speak, is a perpetual factory of idols."[9] Adam and Eve's fall left humanity incapacitated to do what is right and pleasing before God, in thought and action. Every parent will agree that they never had to teach their kids to disobey! The only way out of our spiral of death and destruction is for God to refashion and restore his image within us. The Old Testament bears witness to the continued failure of Israel's kings, who are created in God's image, to rule on behalf of God and manifest justice on the earth. Humanity's natural inclination is to defile that which is holy, cast into chaos that which is in order, twist and pervert the truth, and worship and adore the creation instead of the Creator.

THE PROMISE OF ETERNAL LIFE
UPON PERFECT OBEDIENCE

Like the covenant made with Adam and Eve, the covenant God makes with Israel appears to promise eternal life in the new creation upon perfect obedience. If Israel perfectly obeys God by fulfilling their covenantal obligations to rule over all forms of rebellion, embody the divine law, and mediate God's presence to the nations, then God will transform their bodies and all of creation. The "covenant of works" that is made between God and the first couple in the garden is, to some extent, rehearsed at Sinai.[10] The result of perfect obedience is what is depicted in Revelation 21–22—the descent of God in the new creation. The goal of Genesis 1–2 hasn't been altered. From the very beginning, God has always intended on dwelling intimately with a perfected humanity in a perfected environment.

At Sinai, God offers Israel eternal life in the new creation if they succeed (Leviticus 18:5; Deuteronomy 4:1; Ezekiel 18:9; 20:11; Matthew 19:17; Romans 2:13; 7:10; 10:5; Galatians 3:12). But like Adam and Eve, Israel broke God's law

---

[9]John Calvin, *Institutes of the Christian Religion*, ed. John T. McNeill, trans. Ford Lewis Battles (Louisville: Westminster John Knox, 1960), 1.11.8.

[10]As Meredith G. Kline astutely points out, when God sovereignly and graciously ratifies a covenant himself, it falls into the category of "grace" (e.g., Abraham), but when a human ratifies the covenant through an oath, the covenant falls into the category of "works" (*Kingdom Prologue: Genesis Foundations for a Covenantal Worldview* [Eugene, OR: Wipf & Stock, 2006], 5). Here at Sinai, the covenant is ratified by the Israelites, so we should understand the Mosaic covenant largely within the classification of a covenant of works.

and forfeited the promise of life. The nation broke God's law because they, like all of humanity, are affected by Adam and Eve's fall. From the outset, the Israelites *cannot* obey the law perfectly. This is no mere do-over for humanity. Nevertheless, despite the legitimate offer made by God, Israel fails to adhere to the stipulations of the covenant. Although Israel is stiffed-necked, the covenant is renewed in Exodus 34 with a new set of stone tablets (Exodus 34:1).

At some level, the Mosaic law is a general rehearsal or, as some theologians call it, a "republication" of the covenant of works.[11] The nature of the covenant with Moses is, like the agreement with Adam and Eve, conditional. *If* Israel obeys perfectly, *then* God will bless them. As I outlined above, Israel failed to live up to their end of the covenant. At several key passages in the Pentateuch, the hope of Israel is grounded not in the conditional covenant at Sinai, since they cannot uphold their end of the bargain, but in the unconditional covenant with Abraham (e.g., Leviticus 26:42; Numbers 24:17; Deuteronomy 4:31).[12]

Nevertheless, within the law of Moses, God offers the hope of a coming deliverer and a once-for-all atoning sacrifice. This future servant will perfectly fulfill the Adamic commission, meeting all of God's demands. Those within the nation of Israel under the Mosaic covenant, who embrace the Lord by faith and trust in these promises of redemption, are converted. God gives them a new heart and restores their image. One could say that some Israelites are "born into the 'covenant of works' and are brought into the 'covenant of grace.'"[13]

---

[11]Scholars vigorously debate the nature of the Mosaic covenant and its relationship to God's covenants with prefall Adam (covenant of works) and postfall Adam (covenant of grace). On the one hand, many theologians argue that the Mosaic covenant is strictly an expression of the covenant of grace (e.g., John Murray, *The Covenant of Grace: A Biblico-theological Study* [Phillipsburg, NJ: P&R, 1987]). However, the covenant at Sinai remained largely conditional, based on the nation's obedience. As mentioned above, the parallels between the creation of Adam in the garden and the formation of Israel at Sinai are extensive. Thus, some scholars argue, and I think rightly so, that the Mosaic covenant is generally but not an exact reiteration of the covenant of works (e.g., Michael Horton, *God of Promise: Introducing Covenant Theology* [Grand Rapids: Baker Books, 2006]; Kline, *Kingdom Prologue*). The difference between the covenants made with Adam and Israel is twofold: (1) the nature of Israel's "works" are not meritorious because the Israelites are in a postfall era; (2) elements of the covenant of grace are found in the Mosaic covenant—God graciously brought Israel out of Egypt, initiated a covenant relationship with them, and so on (see WCF 7.5).

[12]Stephen G. Dempster, *Dominion and Dynasty: A Theology of the Hebrew Bible*, NSBT 15 (Downers Grove, IL: IVP Academic, 2003), 104-17.

[13]R. Michael Allen, *Reformed Theology* (New York: T&T Clark, 2010), 44.

THE PROMISE OF REDEMPTION

With the fall of Israel at Sinai, a key question lingers: Has God's intention for humanity changed? Will the entire earth be filled with kings, prophets, and priests that glorify his name? How can a holy God dwell with an unholy people? The answer is twofold: the coming redeemer and Israel's temple. Embedded within Israel's law and throughout the Pentateuch, hope remains for a future individual to fill Adam's and Israel's shoes who will obey where they did not (see Genesis 3:15). Also, within the sacrificial system there is an expectation that God will one day send the ultimate sacrifice who will bear the sins of God's people. The task of this individual is both active and passive. The active component fulfills God's original commission to Adam, and the passive component satisfies God's wrath by bearing the sins of his people. In the next chapter, we will explore this coming redeemer in more detail and how his ministry restores the image of the people of God.

The other critical dimension to God's redemption is the mobile tabernacle and the permanent temple. Israel's tabernacle and temple provide the way in which God will dwell with humanity and ensure that his promises are met. I will now briefly survey the three main tiers of the tabernacle/temple and then explain their significance in relation to being created in God's image.

The tabernacle and temple models of the cosmos. Moses constructed the mobile sanctuary that was used in the wilderness wanderings, and Solomon later built a permanent structure in Jerusalem. Both structures were composed of three parts: the outer courts, the holy place, and the holy of holies. Each tier corresponded to a cosmic reality: the outer courts symbolized the earth (Exodus 20:24-25; 1 Kings 7:23-25), the holy place signified the visible heavens (Genesis 1:14; Exodus 25:8-9), and the holy of holies represented the invisible heavens, where God dwells with his angels (Exodus 25:18-22; Isaiah 6:1-7).[14]

The structure of the temple is symbolic of God's ultimate intention to dwell intimately with his people and creation. By arranging the temple in a three-tiered structure, from the most holy to the least holy, God discloses his plan

---

[14]L. Michael Morales, *Who Shall Ascend the Mountain of the Lord? A Biblical Theology of the Book of Leviticus*, NSBT 37 (Downers Grove, IL: IVP Academic, 2015), 101.

of redemption. The miniature cosmos looks up and looks forward. It looks up as it corresponds to the cosmos, and it looks forward as it corresponds to humanity's future redemption.

The physical temple is simply a model of something greater to come. While it's true that God dwelt in the holy of holies, the Israelites only experienced God in part. All of heaven and earth were ultimately designed to house the Lord's glory. Isaiah 66:1 expresses this reality:

This is what the LORD says:

"*Heaven is my throne,*
    and the earth is my footstool.
Where is the house you will build for me?
    Where will my resting place be?*" (see also Psalm 78:69)

God's special, glorious presence remains sequestered in the back room of the temple. The cosmic design of the temple indicates that this sequestered presence will eventually break out from the heavenly holy of holies and fill every nook and cranny of the new cosmos. The Israelites were to look on the tabernacle and contemplate its significance for their daily lives and for their future inheritance in the new creation. In symbolic form, it narrates God's purpose for humanity and creation. What does the miniature cosmic temple have to do with bearing God's image? The story of the temple is the story of God's people. Recall that, from the very beginning, images are created to dwell in God's presence. The closer we are to God's glory, the more our divine image glows, enabling us to function fully as kings, priests, and prophets.

This principle is illustrated when Moses descends from the top of Mount Sinai, the holy of holies. On the heels of Israel's fashioning a golden calf and misunderstanding their role in bearing God's image, Moses descends from the mountain as one who rightly grasps what being created in God's image entails—enjoying God's glory and mediating it to others.[15] The glory of the Lord cannot be mediated by a golden calf or anything else besides humans. Indeed, God's presence was so glorious and magnificent that it rubbed off on

---

[15]R. W. L. Moberly, *At the Mountain of God: Story and Theology in Exodus 32–34*, JSOTSup 22 (Sheffield: Sheffield Academic Press, 1983), 108.

Moses, leaving him with a radiant face (Exodus 34:30). Moses was exemplary in how he imaged God on Sinai.

On the wilderness journey, Israel is camped around the tabernacle with the twelve tribes arranged to the north, south, east, and west (Numbers 2). Sandwiched between the twelve tribes, the Levites function as a buffer between the tabernacle and the nation in order to prevent God's wrath from falling on the Israelite community (Numbers 1:53). As Israel marches through the dusty wilderness for the next forty years, they will recognize God's gracious presence in their midst. It is no mirage. It is a cosmic interruption in the desert. It is Eden in a dry and barren land—tangible evidence of God's covenant and his constant care in their lives. His presence is an ever-present reality that nourishes all those who bear his image (Numbers 24:5-9).

Fewer memories are as vivid in my mind as my wedding day. On a hot July day in the summer of 2005, my wife and I made a lifelong commitment to one another. I remember it like it was yesterday. My wedding ring is a tangible expression of our love and commitment. Whenever I look at it or feel it on my hand, I think about my wife. The same could be said of Israel's tabernacle: when the Israelites looked at the structure standing in the midst of their camp, they were to think about the goodness of God, his loyalty to them, and his intention to one day dwell with them in the new creation. The entire cosmos is destined to become a gigantic holy of holies, wherein God's people will enjoy a perfected image.

The splintering of the offices. In the first chapter, we explored how God created Adam and Eve in his image to reflect and refract the three offices of king, priest, and prophet. We saw in the present chapter how the book of Exodus juxtaposes the creation of Adam and Eve in the garden with the creation of Israel at Sinai. The nation of Israel was created to function as a corporate king, priest, and prophet. Just as the fall of Adam and Eve altered how they were to fulfill Genesis 1:28, so too the fall of Israel changed how they manifested God's presence on the earth. The divine purpose remains the same—God and humanity dwelling with one another in the new creation— but what did change was how that would be accomplished. Sin affects how the divine commission will be fulfilled.

One concrete effect of Israel's sin is the splintering of the offices of king, priest, and prophet. All three offices were united with Adam and Eve in the garden and with Israel at Sinai. But as Israel's story unfolds, we learn that the three offices begin to splinter. Every Israelite bears God's image, and thus possesses the offices of king, priest, and prophet. Yet the Mosaic covenant formalizes a threefold distinction and organizes them into three distinct offices.

The book of Deuteronomy narrates Moses' instructions to the second generation of Israelites as they are gathered on the plains of Moab, about to occupy the land of Canaan. According to Deuteronomy 17–18, Moses outlines the responsibilities of Israel's kings (Deuteronomy 17:14-20), priests (Deuteronomy 18:1-8), and prophets (Deuteronomy 18:14-22). Israel's priests are responsible for maintaining the purity of the sanctuary through rituals and sacrifices and for representing the entire nation as they minister before the Lord. The priests of Israel embody what Israel should be and one day will be. They are, as Numbers 3:11 states, "in place of all the firstborn of the Israelites." The kings of Israel are charged with keeping peace in the land and driving out all forms of rebellion. Her prophets are commanded to model godly living and to receive God's law and speak it faithfully to the nation. All three offices are designed to work seamlessly with one another and thus preserve God's presence in the midst of Israel.

WHO IS ISRAEL?

At this point in our discussion of Israel, I need to clarify the meaning of the term *Israel*. Does the term *Israel* primarily denote an *ethnic* relationship between Abraham and his descendants? Or does it primarily refer to a spiritual status between God and his people? The name *Israel* first occurs immediately following Jacob's wrestling the angel in Genesis 32:28. The angel gives the patriarch that name because he "struggled with God and with humans and [has] overcome" (Genesis 32:28). Even the name *Israel* probably means "God fights" or "God struggles."[16] As many commentators argue, this

---

[16]Gordon J. Wenham, *Genesis 16–50*, WBC 2 (Waco, TX: Word, 1994), 296-97.

event in Jacob's life signals a new redemptive phase in his life. The name change demonstrates a fundamental shift in how Jacob relates to God. Hans LaRondelle explains, "The name 'Israel' from the beginning symbolizes a personal relation of reconciliation with God. The rest of Holy Scripture never loses sight of this sacred root of the name."[17]

Certainly, the Old Testament employs the term *Israel* to refer to a physical or ethnic dimension to the people of God, but the spiritual dimension remains paramount. To be part of Israel means to be part of the covenant community. The Old Testament is filled with examples of non-Israelites, or Gentiles, joining the covenant community and receiving an inheritance in the land. Their relationship to the covenant is determined ultimately by faith in God's promises.

Many examples could be given, but two will suffice. Psalm 87:2-6 speaks of Gentiles being "born" in Zion at the very end of history and becoming indistinguishable from ethnic Israelites:

> The LORD loves the gates of Zion
> > more than all the other dwellings of Jacob.
> Glorious things are said of you,
> > city of God:
> "I will record *Rahab and Babylon*
> > among those who acknowledge me—
> *Philistia too, and Tyre, along with Cush—*
> > and will say, '*This one was born in Zion.*'"
> Indeed, of Zion it will be said,
> > "This one and that one were born in her,
> > and the Most High himself will establish her."
> The LORD will write in the register of the peoples:
> > "This one was born in Zion."

The psalmist predicts that some of Israel's neighbors—Egypt, Babylon, Philistia, Tyre, and Cush—will be considered full-blown citizens of the covenant community at the very end of history. Both native Israelites and Gentiles will bear the honorable title "born of Zion." That is, Gentiles will one day be called

---

[17]Hans K. LaRondelle, *The Israel of God in Prophecy: Principles of Prophetic Interpretation* (Berrien Springs, MI: Andrews University Press, 1983), 82.

"Israel." The point is that the term Israel is not ultimately ethnic in nature but spiritual.[18]

The second example is found in Isaiah 19, where the prophet anticipates the restoration of the nations at the very end of history. According to Isaiah 19:25, "The LORD Almighty will bless them [Egypt and Assyria], saying, 'Blessed be Egypt my people, Assyria my handiwork, and Israel my inheritance.'" Throughout the Old Testament, Israel is often described as being God's "people" (Psalm 100:3), his "handiwork" (Isaiah 29:23; 64:8), and his "inheritance" (Deuteronomy 9:26; 32:9). In a striking manner, Isaiah applies such language to Egypt and Assyria! The conclusion is that the remnant within all three nations—Egypt, Assyria, and Israel—are considered to be part of God's covenant community (Isaiah 19:24).

What does this discussion of the nature of Israel have to do with the image of God? When God graciously restores an individual's image, that person becomes part of the true covenant community and thus a member of "true Israel." The effect of a right relationship with God is admittance in the people of God. Vertical then horizontal. What fundamentally defines a person is their relationship to God, not their DNA. This explains why the Old Testament, through and through, distinguishes between the nation of Israel (the majority) and the remnant of Israel (the minority). The majority is rebellious and only participates in the Mosaic covenant in an external sense (offering sacrifices, keeping dietary restrictions, etc.); the majority of the nation's heart remains unchanged. But the remnant *within* the nation relates to the covenant community in a spiritual way and participates within the covenant of grace (Genesis 3:15). The remnant enjoys a restored image and has the ability, by God's grace, to obey, albeit imperfectly, the law of Moses internally and externally.

---

[18]Gentiles becoming part of Israel is therefore part of Old Testament prophecy. Old Testament prophets expected that Gentiles would indeed join Israel in the latter days and be declared part of true Israel. This is a critical point, one that is often overlooked in contemporary discussions of dispensationalism. For example, Michael J. Vlach has recently argued that "Israel of the Old Testament consists of the ethnic descendants of Abraham. . . . There is no transformation or transcending of the concept of Israel. There is no enlargement or expansion of Israel to include Gentiles" (*Dispensationalism: Essential Beliefs and Common Myths*, rev. ed. [Los Angeles: Theological Studies Press, 2017], 77).

CONCLUSION AND APPLICATION

One particular tagline nicely summarizes this chapter—history repeats itself. Israel, as a corporate Adam, was charged with fulfilling their God-given identity. They were to rule over all rebellion in the Promised Land and bring everything under God's indomitable rule, mediate his presence to the nations, and embody his law. But despite their commitment to upholding their aspect of the covenant, they immediate broke it.

According to Romans 1:18, the behavior of the Gentiles is indistinct from the behavior of the idolatrous Israelites at Sinai. Gentiles, too, have failed to worship the Creator and have turned to worshiping figurative idols. Unbelieving Gentiles believed the lie that knowledge of salvation could be attained outside of the sphere of God, outside his revelation. They were convinced that they could indeed procure independence from him (Romans 1:21). Adam and Eve's fall is repeated here in the behavior of Gentiles. They worshiped creation instead of the Creator, a behavior that is antithetical to being in God's image. Humanity is designed to worship only God, but because of Adam and Eve's rebellion, humanity is ensnared in a spiral of idolatrous behavior. Lack of trust in God's Word inevitably leads to trust in ourselves. When we trust ourselves, we commit idolatry. When we commit idolatry, we conform to our idols. When we conform to our idols, we become enslaved to them. Left to ourselves, there's no way out.

In a very real sense, when we sin, we repeat the fall of Adam and Eve and the fall of the nation of Israel. The story always remains the same. It wasn't until the coming of Christ that the pattern was broken. Though he was tempted just like Adam and Eve and the nation of Israel, he remained faithful. His faithfulness is passed on to those who trust in him. It is only through Christ's perfect life that we are freed from our idolatry and escape the wrath of God. Christ bore the unfaithful, idolatrous behavior of his people so that we could become perfectly restored images in the sight of God. We would do well to remind ourselves daily of the seriousness of our sin and of the grace that is found in Christ's work on our behalf.

Another relevant area of application is the nature of Israel and what it means to be a child of the King. Fundamentally, our relationship with God and his people rests not on our DNA but on our image. Those who enjoy a fundamentally restored image are considered part of "true Israel." When God changed Jacob's name to Israel his DNA wasn't altered like a Marvel superhero. The name Israel symbolized a new dimension of Jacob's relationship with God, signaling divine blessing on him (Genesis 32:29). Likewise, when we trust in Christ for our salvation, we receive God's covenantal blessing by becoming a legitimate child of Jacob, or Israel.

Does ethnicity matter at all, then? The apostle Paul takes up this precise line of questioning in Romans 3:1-2 and Romans 9:4-5:

> What advantage, then, is there in being a Jew, or what value is there in circumcision? Much in every way! First of all, the Jews have been entrusted with the very words of God.
>
> Theirs is the adoption to sonship; theirs the divine glory, the covenants, the receiving of the law, the temple worship and the promises. Theirs are the patriarchs, and from them is traced the human ancestry of the Messiah, who is God over all, forever praised!

Here Paul is underscoring Israel's unique status in contrast to other nations. God graciously chose the Israelites to be his people. Though ethnicity is not ultimately a determining factor in one's relationship with God (Romans 2:28-29; 9:6), he did sovereignly and graciously cut a covenant with a particular people group. He made a formal agreement with the nation of Israel, gave them his law and a land, and dwelled in the midst of them. So, on the one hand, Israel as a people group possesses unique privileges. But on the other, Israel is part of a much larger story—God's commitment to securing a people group from all ethnicities for himself and dwelling intimately with them. Adam, Noah, Abraham, Israel, and the church are all part of the same covenant community within the different epochs of biblical history.

RECOMMENDED READING

Belcher, Richard P., Jr. *Prophet, Priest, and King: Roles of Christ in the Bible and Our Roles Today*. Phillipsburg, NJ: P&R, 2016.

Kline, Meredith G. *Kingdom Prologue: Genesis Foundations for a Covenantal Worldview*. Eugene, OR: Wipf & Stock, 2006.

LaRondelle, Hans K. *The Israel of God in Prophecy: Principles of Prophetic Interpretation*. Berrien Springs, MI: Andrews University Press, 1983.

Martin, Oren R. *Bound for the Promised Land: The Land Promise in God's Redemptive Plan*. NSBT 34. Downers Grove, IL: IVP Academic, 2015.

Morales, L. Michael. *Who Shall Ascend the Mountain of the Lord? A Biblical Theology of the Book of Leviticus*. NSBT 37. Downers Grove, IL: IVP Academic, 2015.

Chapter Four

ISRAEL'S RESTORATION
IN THE "LATTER DAYS"

HAVING SKETCHED THE FALL of Adam and Israel in the previous chapters, I will now take a look at the future success of an individual coming at the very end of history. The Old Testament writers and prophets all the way back to Genesis 1–3 foresaw a time when the final redemption of God's people and creation would emerge. This last epoch in Israel's story was to take place at the very end of history. This period entails God's greatest act of redemption, but instead of repeating the fall of Adam and Israel, a future righteous figure will arrive on the scene and succeed in obeying the divine commission and resisting sin and temptation. The success of this individual will secure God's decisive act of redeeming creation and humanity in the new heavens and earth. At that point, God will descend from heaven and dwell with redeemed humanity in the new creation for all of eternity.

It is here where biblical eschatology comes to the fore. In the last several decades, eschatology has been a hot-button issue in the church and even in pop culture. The dispensational *Left Behind* series has sold over 80 million copies and spawned an entire new genre of video games, movies, and graphic novels. *Left Behind* has been influential in how we read our Bibles and think about Israel and the end times. It has also thrown a lot of people into confusion. I've heard more than a few people quip that they are "pan-millennialists" because everything will "pan out" in the future. Eschatological agnosticism, though, can wreak havoc on some important Christian doctrines.

A more sober, biblical understanding of eschatology is needed. Our English term *eschatology* comes from two Greek words: *eschatos* (last) and *logos* (word). So eschatology is the study of the "last things." The final phase of redemption should be considered eschatological, as it takes place at the very end of history. The Old Testament uses the phrase "latter days" or the "last days" to refer to this final period of Israel's history (e.g., Genesis 49:1; Numbers 24:14; Daniel 2:28-29, 45). All the events that take place within this period, whether acts of judgment or restoration, are eschatological. Like a seed germinating, sprouting, and eventually growing into a tree, the Old Testament writings begin with an eschatological seed in Genesis 1–3 and have developed into a vast tree by the close of the canon. The period of the "latter days" is not unrelated to or disconnected from the remainder of the Old Testament. It is the climax of Israel's story.

This present chapter covers a great deal of redemptive-historical ground, but I thought it best to include a chapter on the eschatological dimension of the people of God. Though many popular volumes on the image of God tend to downplay the significance of eschatology, it's critical for a right understanding of what it means to be part of the people of God. Below I will outline the nature of the Messiah's image and how his success leads to the restoration of God's people. As the second Adam and true Israel, this figure will conquer God's enemies, mediate his presences to the nations, and embody divine truth. In sum, his obedience leads to the restoration of the covenant community.

THE ARRIVAL OF THE ANTI-PRIEST, ANTI-KING, AND ANTI-PROPHET

An effect of the fall on Adam and Eve was the self-destructive nature of the perverted image of God. I noted in chapter two that Adam and Eve began to be conformed into the image of the serpent and embody his traits. They attempted to deceive God in the same way the serpent deceived them (Genesis 3:12-13). Cain, too, instead of ruling over sin, ruled over his brother and killed him (Genesis 4:7-9). In much of the remaining Old Testament material, we sadly discover the destructive nature of humanity's kingly, priestly, and prophetic offices. The ungodly line, as anti-kings, will rule viciously by abusing one another and the created order. These descendants, as anti-priests, will also defile the created order and worship everything but the one true God. The ungodly line, as anti-prophets, will deceive and embody all teaching that is hostile to God.

Within the final phase of Israel's history, an individual will emerge on the scene who fully embodies all three of these self-destructive traits. He is the anti-messiah. Genesis 3:15 sets forth the broad trajectory of warfare between the godly and ungodly descendants of Adam:

And I will put *enmity*
　　between you and the woman,
　　and between your offspring and hers;
he will crush your head,
　　and you will strike his heel. (Genesis 3:15)

Meredith Kline summarizes the thrust of Genesis 3:15 this way: "The enmity between the serpent's seed and the woman's seed was that of rival claimants for the ultimate possession of the world."[1]

Within the Pentateuch, God's people are often oppressed, physically and spiritually. Cain, the first descendant of Adam and Eve, murdered his brother Abel (Genesis 4:6-10). Pharaoh enslaved Israel and attempted to murder the baby males of Israel (Exodus 2:15-16). As Israel wandered in the desert, the Amorites waged war against them (Numbers 21:21-30). And once the nation entered the Promised Land, they were beset with great opposition. Intertwined with physical opposition is false teaching. False prophets are a considerable part of Israel's story. Deuteronomy lays out the criteria for determining whether a prophet is genuine (Deuteronomy 18:22),

[1]Meredith G. Kline, *Kingdom Prologue: Genesis Foundations for a Covenantal Worldview* (Eugene, OR: Wipf & Stock, 2006), 214.

yet false prophets often misled the nation, causing many within the nation to stumble (Numbers 22–25; 1 Kings 18:19-40; Jeremiah 23:16-18; Ezekiel 13:3).

The idea of an end-time antagonist, a figure who will oppress and deceive the covenant community in the "latter days," begins to emerge within the prophetic corpus of the Old Testament. By far the most detailed discussion of this end-time oppressor appears in the book of Daniel, particularly Daniel 11–12. According to Daniel 11, an end-time attack on Israel will manifest itself in two ways. An opponent will persecute righteous Israelites. Daniel 11:31 says, "His armed forces will rise up *to desecrate the temple fortress and will abolish the daily sacrifice*. Then they will set up the abomination that causes desolation" (cf. Daniel 2:8, 11, 25; 8:9-12; Isaiah 14:12-14). Here the enemy is presented as an anti-priest, who is postured against the temple precinct. Instead of mediating God's presence and keeping out all unclean things within the sanctuary, the antagonist pollutes God's temple. Daniel 11:33-35 describes the attack against the "wise" within the covenant community: "Those who are wise will instruct many, though for a time *they will fall by the sword or be burned or captured or plundered*" (Daniel 11:33). The anti-king wages warfare against God's people. Instead of ruling over Israel's enemies, the antagonist rules over the covenant community.

Finally, Israel's latter-day enemy, as the anti-prophet, will also deceive some within the Israelite community through enticing speech. His deception results in the fact that some within the covenant community "forsake the holy covenant" (Daniel 11:30). His influence through flattery also extends to those "who have violated the covenant" such that they become even more godless (Daniel 11:32), they compromise, and they foster deception among others. Daniel 11:34 reveals that "many who are not sincere will join them [the faithful]." These Israelites will claim to be faithful to God's law but will, in reality, be unfaithful.

ISRAEL'S NEW EXODUS

The appearance of Israel's antagonist sets the stage for God's final act of redemption for Israel. When it appears that the anti-messiah will emerge victorious, pushing Israel to the precipice of collapse, God will intervene and deliver his people. Old Testament prophets viewed the redemption of Israel at the very end of history as a new or second exodus. Israel's redemption from Egypt became a prophetic pattern or type for Israel's final and consummate redemption. The prophets looked back to God's dealing with Israel in the past and predicted that God would repeat his redemption of Israel. This time around, though, God would fully deliver Israel. The second exodus would be greater than the first.

The book of Isaiah, perhaps more than any other Old Testament book, portrays the restoration of Israel from Babylon as a second exodus. The Lord will manifest his glory (Isaiah 40:5 / Exodus 16:7, 10; 24:16) and repeat the mountaintop experience at Sinai (Isaiah 64:1-3 / Exodus 19:1-25). God, like in the first exodus, will lead Israel through water:

> When you pass through the waters,
>   I will be with you;
> and when you pass through the rivers,
>   they will not sweep over you. (Isaiah 43:2; cf. Isaiah 51:9-11 /
>   Exodus 13:17–14:31)

He even promises to guide Israel through the wilderness, like he originally did in a cloud, both at the front and at the rear of the caravan:

> But you will not leave in haste,
>   or go in flight;
> For the LORD will go before you,
>   the God of Israel will be your rear guard. (Isaiah 52:12; cf. Isaiah 40:11 /
>   Exodus 13:21-22)

As the Lord provided food and water in the first exodus, so too in the second:

> Along the roads they will feed,
> And their pasture will be on all bare heights.
> They will not hunger or thirst,
> Nor will the scorching heat or sun strike them down;
> For He who has compassion on them will lead them
> and will guide them to springs of water. (Isaiah 49:9-10 /
>   Numbers 10:11-32:42 NASB)

Within this framework of the second exodus, the prophets, especially Isaiah, explain *how* the exodus will take place—through the faithfulness of an individual. A figure will arise within Israel in the latter days who will trigger Israel's redemption. The famous "servant" of Isaiah will be instrumental in delivering Israel from Babylonian captivity (Isaiah 42:1-9; 49:1-6; 50:4-9; 52:13–53:12). In the perfect image of God, the Messiah will retrace Adam and Israel's steps and succeed where they failed. Their faithlessness anticipated his faithfulness. The Messiah's obedience leads to the restoration of the covenant community's image. His perfect image fashions a perfected image in the hearts of God's people. The coming Adam will create a community of perfected Adams.

THE ARRIVAL OF THE FAITHFUL KING, PRIEST, AND PROPHET

Many Old Testament passages speak or at least hint at a coming Adam figure who will deliver Israel and redeem her from her plight. The term *messiah* means "anointed one." The verb "to anoint" connotes being set apart for a distinct purpose. We find this word used in contexts discussing the tabernacle and the altar (Exodus 40:9-11). The noun form is applied to priests (Leviticus 4:3; 1 Samuel 2:35) and kings (e.g., 1 Samuel 24:6; 26:11) and, in particular, current and future rulers of Israel (e.g., Psalm 2:2; 18:50). The book of Daniel anticipates an end-time ruler who will judge the pagan nations and usher in God's eternal kingdom (Daniel 2:35, 44-45; 7:13-14). Taken together, the Old Testament collectively speaks of an individual who is "anointed" for a specific purpose—ruling over Israel and the nations and redeeming all of creation.

We have already seen how Genesis 3:15 sets the stage for the development of a messianic figure, albeit in seed form:

> And I will put enmity
>> between you and the woman,
>> and between your offspring and hers;
> *he will crush your head,*
>> and you will strike his heel. (Genesis 3:15)

One of the promises God makes to the original couple is that their descendants will form two lines of progeny, a godly and an ungodly seed, and these two will continually wage war with one another. One of their descendants, though, will eventually "bruise" or "crush" the head of the serpent.

At the end of Genesis, Jacob blesses his twelve sons, and Judah receives a particularly special blessing:

> Judah . . .
>> your hand will be on the neck of your enemies. . . .
> The scepter will not depart from Judah,
>> nor the ruler's staff from between his feet,
> until he to whom it belongs shall come,
>> and *the obedience of the nations* shall be his. (Genesis 49:8-10)

According to this passage, in the "latter days" (Genesis 49:1; NIV: "days to come") a ruler will descend from the tribe of Judah and conquer Israel's enemies. The result of this decisive victory is that the nations and Israel will pay obeisance to him. In Numbers 24:17, a "star" will come from Jacob in the "latter days" (Numbers 24:14) who will "crush the foreheads of Moab"—a longtime enemy of Israel.

God makes a covenant with David in 2 Samuel 7, wherein he promises to maintain a Davidic ruler in Jerusalem: "I will raise up your offspring to succeed you . . . *and I will establish his kingdom.* He is the one who will build a house for my Name, *and I will establish the throne of his kingdom forever*" (2 Samuel 7:12-13). This ruler will not only establish God's eternal kingdom but also build God's temple, or "house."

The book of Isaiah prophesies that a latter-day ruler of Israel will eliminate Israel's enemies and rule with righteousness and wisdom. Isaiah 11:1-5 describes this messianic figure, the "branch," in some detail:

> A shoot will come up from the stump of Jesse;
>> from his roots a Branch will bear fruit. . . .
> But with righteousness he will judge the needy. . . .
> *He will strike the earth with the rod of his mouth,*
>> and with the breath of his lips *he will slay the wicked.*
>> (see also Isaiah 9:6-7)

It is likely that this ruler should be identified with the suffering servant in the later portions of Isaiah, who brings about the release of Israel from Babylonian captivity and restores the righteous remnant (Isaiah 42:1-9; 49:1-6; 50:4-9; 52:13–53:12).

The coming of a righteous deliverer is central to the book of Daniel, especially, Daniel 2 and Daniel 7. The description of an end-time ruler in Daniel 2 is quite significant given the immediate context. The narrative in Daniel 2–3 describes one of the most grandiose examples of idolatry in the entire Bible. Nebuchadnezzar dreams of a colossus, and only Daniel can unlock the dream's full interpretation. The statue is composed of four parts (Daniel 2:31-35), and each part symbolizes a particular kingdom (Daniel 2:36-44). The dream climaxes in the arrival of a "rock cut out of a mountain" that smashes the statue (Daniel 2:44-45). Despite being in a position to rule wisely over "all mankind and the beasts of the field and the birds in the sky" (Daniel 2:38; cf. Genesis 1:27-28), Nebuchadnezzar audaciously proceeds to construct the colossus in the following chapter.

The statue in his dream is composed of three different materials, and the head, symbolizing the Babylonian Empire, is manufactured out of gold. In Daniel 3, though, the entire image is made from gold! The golden image Nebuchadnezzar fashions symbolizes the magnificence and power of *his* kingdom.

The parallels between Daniel 2–3 and Genesis 1–3 are staggering:

- In Genesis 1–2, God, as sovereign creator, fashions humanity in his image, whereas in Daniel 3, Nebuchadnezzar, as a false god, creates an image in his likeness.

- In Genesis 1–2, God creates Adam and Eve to mediate his rule over the earth, whereas in Daniel 3, Nebuchadnezzar is attempting to mediate his rule over the earth. (King)

- In Genesis 1–2, God commands Adam and Eve to worship only him, whereas in Daniel 3, Nebuchadnezzar orders humanity to worship the statue. (Priest)

- In Genesis 1–2, God is the supreme fountain of truth, whereas in Daniel 3, Nebuchadnezzar claims to be the lawgiver. (Prophet)

The point is hard to miss: Nebuchadnezzar views himself as god, attempting to act like the creator of the cosmos. Someone made in God's image (Nebuchadnezzar) creates an image of himself so that other images can worship him.[2] Irony runs thick here. King Nebuchadnezzar is the anti-image par excellence. God, though, will not let such idolatry run rampant. Nebuchadnezzar will eventually be transformed into a grotesque beast (a symbol for his kingdom), the very thing he worshiped (Daniel 4:1-37; cf. 7:3-4). Meanwhile Daniel 2 predicts the arrival of a "rock cut out of a mountain," a reference to the Messiah. Unlike the statue that is fashioned by humanity, this "rock" is pristinely fashioned by God. The long-awaited Messiah will be God's instrument in overthrowing idolatry.

We saw in the previous chapters how Genesis 1-3 portrays Adam as a king, priest, and prophet. Adam was to rule over the created order, mediate God's presence on earth, and teach and obey God's commandments. But the fall split these three aspects of Adam's identity into three distinct offices (see Deuteronomy 17:14–18:22). Nevertheless, the Old Testament envisions the three offices coalescing in a future ruler and in all of God's people in the "latter days." There are even several instances of Old Testament individuals combining the offices in their behavior. Moses was certainly one of the first to display qualities of all three offices (see Genesis 14:18-20). He ruled over Israel, mediated God's presence to the Israelites, and communicated God's law to them. David, who ruled over the united monarchy, spoke often about entering God's temple (e.g., Psalm 63), even donned an ephod (2 Samuel 6:14), and partook of the bread in the holy place (1 Samuel 21), acts only permissible for priests. His writing of a good portion of the book of Psalms also testifies to David's prophetic role. Deuteronomy 18:15 predicts the arrival of an endtime prophet within Israel, and Psalm 110 explicitly identifies a future ruler that will be a "priest forever, in the order of Melchizedek" (Psalm 110:4; cf. Zechariah 6:13).

---

[2]Anthony A. Hoekema makes the identical observation when he comments, "In Daniel 3 . . . we read that King Nebuchadnezzar set up an image on the plain of Dura. . . . Though the biblical text does not specifically say so, we may presume that the image was a likeness of Nebuchadnezzar himself, and thus represented the king" (*Created in God's Image* [Grand Rapids: Eerdmans, 1986], 67).

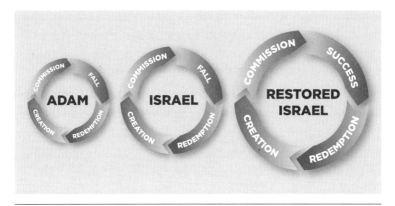

Figure 4.1

The long-awaited Messiah will retrace Adam and Israel's steps but with success (see fig. 4.1). As the righteous king that Adam and Israel should have been, he will be instrumental in the destruction of Israel's antagonist and his allies, the new exodus, the forgiveness of sins, the pouring out of the Spirit, and the dawn of the new creation. The faithfulness of the Messiah, as depicted here in the third cycle, is prophesied to occur in the "latter days" (see fig. 4.2). So, when the Messiah arrives on the scene, we can be confident that the end times have commenced.

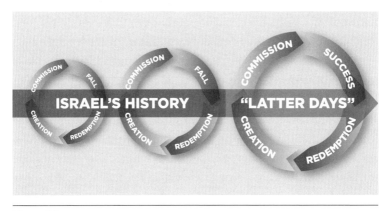

Figure 4.2

The Messiah, a descendant of David, would be the means by which God would establish his eschatological kingdom and vanquish his enemies. In addition to his kingly role, the Messiah will also fill the offices of priest and prophet.

It's unclear, though, at least from the vantage point of the Old Testament authors, how the offices of prophet, priest, and king will merge in a single individual.

RESTORED ISRAEL AS CONQUERING KINGS

The faithfulness of the Messiah will inevitably lead to the restoration of Israel as the true people of God. All of God's people will, at the very end of history, possess a perfected image. They will rule, worship God, and embody truth, like Adam and Israel should have ruled, worshiped God, and embodied truth. We will now take a moment to examine three prominent passages where the Old Testament anticipates the restoration of Israel as a corporate king, priest, and prophet in the "latter days."

Daniel 7 is quite complex but by far one of the most influential passages in the Old Testament. Critical portions of the New Testament are indebted to and shaped by this perplexing chapter. According to Daniel 7, four beasts representing four hostile empires emerge and wage war with one another. The sea is the embodiment of evil and rebellion. Four kingdoms consume one another sequentially—Medo-Persia, Babylon, Greece, and Rome (Daniel 7:3-8). These kingdoms are presented as grotesque, symbolizing their arrogance and destructive nature.

The vision in Daniel 7 then shifts to heaven, where God is depicted as the "Ancient of Days" with white hair, sitting on a heavenly throne with wheels. God then metes out judgment on the four beasts (Daniel 7:11-12). "One like a son of man" comes up to the Ancient of Days on a cloud and is granted the eternal kingdom (Daniel 7:13-14). Throughout the Old Testament, riding on the clouds is reserved for God alone (Exodus 19:9; Psalm 18:11; 68:4; 104:3; Ezekiel 1:4). The Son of Man is probably an enigmatic divine figure,[3] who approaches the Ancient of Days. This Son of Man receives a royal inheritance: "He was *given* authority, glory and sovereign power; all nations and peoples of every language worshiped him. His dominion is an *everlasting dominion* that will not pass away, and his kingdom is one that will never be destroyed" (Daniel 7:14).

Daniel 7 also presents the Son of Man as an Adam figure who has successfully ruled over God's enemies. The language of "man," "beasts," "rule," and "kingdom"

---

[3]Seyoon Kim, *"The Son of Man" as the Son of God: A Selection*, WUNT 30 (Tübingen: J. C. B. Mohr [Paul Siebeck], 1983; repr. Eugene: Wipf & Stock, 2011), 22-25.

recalls Genesis 1–3. But where the first Adam failed to rule over the serpent, the Son of Man rules over the beasts. The Son of Man inherits what the first Adam should have inherited (see Psalm 8:3-8). The result of the Son of Man's success is the eternal kingdom, a kingdom void of wickedness and rebellion.

Perhaps the reason why the heavenly figure is described as "a son of man" stems from the close identification this figure enjoys with Israel. The Son of Man receives "authority, glory and sovereign power," "an everlasting dominion," and a "kingdom" (Daniel 7:14). According to the second half of the vision, the figure of the Son of Man is replaced by the remnant of Israel (Daniel 7:18, 22, 27). The righteous remnant of Israel will "receive the kingdom and will possess it forever" (Daniel 7:18; see Daniel 7:22, 27). In other words, the Son of Man and the remnant of Israel are to be identified with one another. The second portion of the vision identifies the Son of Man as the "holy people" of Israel.

Often in the Old Testament, kings or prominent figures represent the nation or a large group (Joshua 7:1-5; 2 Samuel 21:1; 1 Chronicles 21:1-17). Here the Son of Man represents the righteous Israelites (hence the phrase "son of *man*"). When he conquers the fourth and final beast, his actions are transferred to the group. The remnant is in a position to receive the kingdom, since the Son of Man, their representative, has vanquished their enemy. Conversely, what is true of the righteous Israelites is also true of the Son of Man. For example, Daniel 7:21 says, "As I watched, this horn was *waging war against the holy people and defeating them*." Here the remnant is coming under severe persecution, perhaps suggesting that the Son of Man, too, will suffer.

The point is that God's people benefit from the actions of a single individual. The victory of the Son of Man leads to the saints' possessing the kingdom (Daniel 7:22). The saints benefit from the triumph of the new Adam. Remember that Adam and Eve were created in God's image to manifest his sovereign rule on the earth (Genesis 1:26-28). According to Daniel 7, the triumphant saints have finally appropriated that same rule over God's enemies through the victory of the Son of Man.

Our identity in Christ, our union with him through the Spirit, ensures us that we benefit from his faithful actions. His victory is our victory; his rule is our rule; his obedience is our obedience. Paul states it as follows: "You are in Christ Jesus, who has become for us wisdom from God—that is, our righteousness, holiness and redemption" (1 Corinthians 1:30). What is true of Christ is true of us. This doctrine is the bedrock of our salvation and the assurance of our future life in the new creation.

RESTORED ISRAEL AS MINISTERING PRIESTS

The book of Isaiah contains a wealth of information on Israel's final redemption and her return to the Promised Land. One precious mineral that we can mine is Isaiah's depiction of Israel as the end-time priest to the nations. In Isaiah 40–53 the term *servant* is found nineteen times, describing, on the one hand, the nation of Israel collectively. The nation is unfaithful in carrying out the divine commission to obey God perfectly and to bring his glory to the ends of the earth. On the other hand, an individual "servant" successfully and faithfully obeys God and bears the guilt of Israel (Isaiah 42:1-9; 49:1-13; 50:4-11; 52:13–53:12). Isaiah 55–66 switches to the plural "servants" to designate an obedient group within Israel that identifies with the one faithful "servant."[4] As true Israel, the individual servant stimulates the formation of a faithful remnant, the true, corporate Israel of God.

This servant is also critical in mediating God's presence to the nations. Isaiah 49:3-6 reads, for example,

> You are my servant,
>   Israel. . . .
> It is too small a thing for you to be my *servant*
>   *to restore the tribes of Jacob*
>   and bring back those of Israel I have kept.
> I will also make you *a light for the Gentiles*,
>   that my salvation may reach to the ends of the earth. (cf. Isaiah 42:6)

Isaiah here identifies the servant, a single individual, as Israel, who will be the catalyst for the restoration of an Israelite remnant and usher Gentiles into the covenant community. Though Isaiah doesn't explicitly label the servant figure a priest here, he is at least functioning as one.

---

[4]Daniel J. Brendsel, "*Isaiah Saw His Glory*": *The Use of Isaiah 52–53 in John 12*, BZNW 208 (Berlin: de Gruyter, 2014), 56-60.

Within this broader framework of a single individual restoring a community, Isaiah 61:6 states,

> And you [Israel] will be called *priests of the LORD*,
>   you will be named ministers of our God.
> You will feed on the wealth of nations,
>   and in their riches you will boast.

The individual servant-priest creates a community of priests. Israel's calling as priests to the nations in Exodus 19:6 is finally realized here in Isaiah 61. What Israel failed to do under the old covenant is now being fulfilled in the new covenant. In the previous verse, "strangers" and "foreigners" are beginning to participate in restored Israel (Isaiah 61:5). These Gentiles are not relegated to the fringes of society but participate within Israel as full-blown citizens.

Isaiah 66:18-21 pushes the envelope even further in that it outlines the integration of Gentiles into restored Israel in the "latter days."[5]

> "For I know their works and their thoughts; the time is coming to gather *all nations* and tongues. And they shall come and see My glory. I will set a sign among *them* [faithful Israelites] and will send survivors from them to the nations: Tarshish, Put, Lud, Meshech, Tubal and Javan, to the distant coastlands that have neither heard My fame nor seen My glory. And they will declare My glory among *the nations*. Then they shall bring all your brethren [i.e., who are Gentiles] from all the nations as a grain offering to the LORD, on horses, in chariots, in litters, on mules and on camels, to My holy mountain Jerusalem," says the LORD, "just as the sons of Israel bring their grain offering in a clean vessel to the house of the LORD. I will also take some of them [Gentiles] for *priests and for Levites*," says the LORD. (NASB)

This passage is notoriously tricky, as there is some ambiguity about the identity of "them" in Isaiah 66:19. The pronoun most likely refers to ethnic Israelites who have begun to experience restoration. The following verse then mentions the missionary efforts of restored Jews to the Gentiles, who become "brethren" to the restored Jews (Isaiah 66:20). Though it is not entirely clear to whom the "brethren" refers, in the immediate context, the term probably should be

---

[5]For further discussion of this tricky passage, see G. K. Beale and Benjamin L. Gladd, *Hidden but Now Revealed: A Biblical Theology of Mystery* (Downers Grove, IL: IVP Academic, 2014), 189-91.

identified with the Gentiles from the surrounding nations. If this is correct, we can then paraphrase Isaiah 66:20 in the following manner: "Then they, the restored Israelites, shall bring all your brethren, the Gentiles, from all the nations as a grain offering to the LORD."

We can finally grasp the meaning of Isaiah 66:21. These "brethren" of Isaiah 66:20 are Gentile converts, some of whom God will make as priests over Israel: "I will also take some of them [the Gentiles] for priests and for Levites" (Isaiah 66:21). Apparently, God appoints some Gentiles and Israelites to function, astonishingly, *as priests and Levites* in his end-time temple! If we are on the right track here, then Isaiah 66 teaches that restored Israelites and Gentiles will function as end-time priests within Israel. So, not only will restored Israel, on a corporate priestly level, mediate God's presence to the nations, but the Gentiles will also participate in priestly service to God at the very end of history.

Once again, we've seen the same pattern emerge here in the book of Isaiah that we saw in Daniel 7: the faithfulness of a single individual leads to the restoration of others. According to Isaiah, the faithfulness of the servant leads to the restoration of the remnant. What is true of the individual servant is true of the corporate servants. Just as the individual mediates God's presence to the nations as a priest-king, so too the remnant of Israel mediates God's presence to the surrounding nations. God's commission to Adam and Eve in Genesis 1:28 that the entire earth be filled with his glory has now taken place. The prophet Isaiah envisions the entire earth filled with the glory of the Lord in the new creation, where Israel and the Gentiles worship and minister in awe and wonder.

ISRAEL AS SPIRIT-FILLED PROPHETS

Under the old covenant, the Spirit empowered kings, priests, and prophets to perform their specific duties. The prophet Joel foresaw a time, though, when *all* within Israel would receive the Spirit and serve in the capacity of prophets. Joel prophesies,

> Your sons and daughters will prophesy,
>> your old men will dream dreams,
>> your young men will see visions.
> Even on my servants, both men and women.
>> I will pour out my Spirit in those days. (Joel 2:28-29)

But Joel 2 is part of a larger expectation that began in the early stages of Israel's career. According to Numbers 11, Moses pleads with God to furnish him with leaders to share in the burden of the people (Numbers 11:11, 17). God orders Moses to gather "seventy men from the elders" and "bring them to the tent of meeting, and let them take their stand there with you. Then I will come down and . . . will take of the Spirit who is upon you, and will put Him upon them" (Numbers 11:16-17 NASB). Moses obeys God: "He gathered seventy men of the elders . . . and stationed them around the tent. Then the LORD came down in the cloud . . . and He took of the *Spirit* who was upon him [Moses] and placed Him upon the *seventy elders*. And when the *Spirit* rested upon them, they *prophesied*" (Numbers 11:24-25 NASB). They then stop prophesying, but two elders at another location continue to prophesy. When Joshua hears about this, he asks Moses to stop them. Moses declines, replying, "Would that *all the LORD's people* were *prophets*, that the Lord would put *His Spirit upon them*" (Numbers 11:26-29 NASB).

What began with a wish from Moses transformed into a formal prophecy by the prophet Joel.[6] The Spirit's gifts, formerly restricted to prophets, kings, and priests, are universalized to all of God's people from every race, young and old, male and female. Adam and Eve were responsible for speaking on behalf of God and embodying his truth to one another and their descendants. This expectation is finally realized at the very end of history, when the Spirit is poured out on God's people in the new covenant and they speak truth and only embody his law (Jeremiah 31:33-34; Ezekiel 36:26).

CONCLUSION AND APPLICATION

Eschatology, when rightly understood, can be immensely helpful for understanding our Bibles and the Christian life. The final phase of God's dealings with humanity and creation is not disconnected from the story line of redemption but is the climax. The creation of Adam and Eve in the garden and their responsibility to live in accordance with possessing the divine image prophetically anticipates the "latter days" when the Lord will populate the earth with his people and dwell intimately among them in the new creation.

---

[6]G. K. Beale, *A New Testament Biblical Theology: The Unfolding of the Old Testament in the New* (Grand Rapids: Baker Academic, 2011), 604.

God promises to achieve this goal through a faithful servant, a faithful Adam, who will rule over God's enemies, mediate God's glory, and faithfully embody and teach God's law.

In the following chapters we will learn how the end of history, the "latter days," has begun in the person of Christ. But for now, this chapter reminds us of the importance of trusting in God's promises to redeem humanity and creation. Many of these promises mentioned above, in their original context, were made to Israel either before they entered into Babylonian captivity or during it. It didn't look like what the prophets predicted would transpire. It looked like the Babylonian Empire had the upper hand. Despite what the eyes of the Israelites saw and what their ears heard, the prophets had to plead with Israel to believe their message. Looks can be deceiving.

We too would benefit from this principle. The Bible tells us that we will not win the culture war and that genuine Christianity will be brought to the edge of extinction (see Revelation 11:7-10). In a world that is increasingly becoming hostile toward Christianity, we must rest in God's promises of redemption. Since he has already begun to deliver us from our plight, we are assured that he will finish what he started. Paul says that we "live by faith, not by sight" (2 Corinthians 5:7). The more we read and meditate on God's intractable promises, the more we have confidence in God's power to bring them to pass.

RECOMMENDED READING

Gladd, Benjamin L., and Matthew H. Harmon. *Making All Things New: Inaugurated Eschatology for the Life of the Church*. Grand Rapids: Baker Academic, 2016.

Hoekema, Anthony A. *The Bible and the Future*. Grand Rapids: Eerdmans, 1994.

Riddlebarger, Kim. *The Man of Sin: Uncovering the Truth About the Antichrist*. Grand Rapids: Baker, 2006.

Chapter Five

JESUS AS KING

FOR US TO UNDERSTAND the nature of God's people, their redemption from sin's long-held sway, and what it means to be in the perfected
divine image, we must first grasp Jesus' identity as the true people of God.
As the successful last Adam, Jesus inherits the original commission, a mission
that requires individuals to obey God perfectly, conquer the devil, and expand
God's glorious presence to the ends of the earth. The fall perverted the image
of God in humanity. Instead of reflecting and refracting God on earth and
giving him the glory, sinful humanity selfishly ruled, worshiped idols, and
embodied lies and deceit. Christ retraces Adam's and Israel's steps, but successfully accomplishes what they failed to do.

This chapter falls into two halves: the first section highlights Christ as the
true and faithful Israel, and the second focuses on Christ's kingship in the
Gospels and Paul. But before we probe the nature of Jesus' success, we must
briefly contextualize his ministry in light of Old Testament expectations
concerning the very end of history. He did not function in a redemptive-
historical vacuum. Jesus' ministry, death, and resurrection are eschatological
to the core and operate within the final phase of God's plan of redemption.
The restoration of the people of God into the perfected divine image was
expected to take place at the very end of history.

INAUGURATION OF THE "LATTER DAYS" AND THE RESTORATION OF THE DIVINE IMAGE

According to the New Testament, the period known as the "latter days" in which Israel's enemies are judged and the covenant community is restored at the end of history has now begun in the person of Christ. Indeed, all that the Old Testament foresaw would occur in the end times has begun to be fulfilled in the first coming of Christ and continues until the second coming of Christ. The divine commission to Adam and Eve in Genesis 1:28 is beginning to come to fruition, and God's glory has begun to invade the earth. As the glory of God filled Israel's tabernacle, so too the glory of God dwells in Jesus. The Old Testament end-time expectations of the great tribulation, God's subjugation of the Gentiles, deliverance of Israel from oppressors, Israel's restoration and resurrection, the new covenant, the promised Spirit, the new creation, the new temple, a messianic king, and the establishment of God's kingdom have all been set in motion through Christ's death and resurrection.

The expression "already–not yet" refers to two stages of the fulfillment of the latter days. It is "already" because the latter days have dawned in Christ, but it is "not yet" since the latter days have not consummately arrived. Scholars often use the phrase "inaugurated eschatology" to describe the beginning stage of the latter days.

Christ's life, trials, and particularly his death and resurrection decisively triggered the latter days (see, e.g., Acts 2:17; 1 Corinthians 10:11; Galatians 4:4; Ephesians 1:7-10). These pivotal events inaugurated the new creation and the eternal kingdom. Believers are caught in the "overlap of the ages." Christ has inaugurated the new age, yet the old age and its effects persist. The Old Testament generally did not foresee such an overlap of the ages, since the old age was to give way decisively to the new age. Figure 5.1 graphically depicts the Old Testament's expectation of the end of history. (Note that I have included only some of the more dominant eschatological themes.)

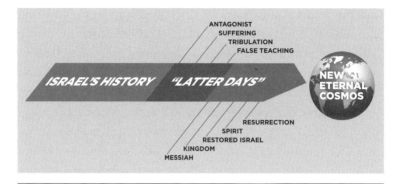

Figure 5.1

The New Testament, however, outlines the schema of fulfillment as seen in figure 5.2.

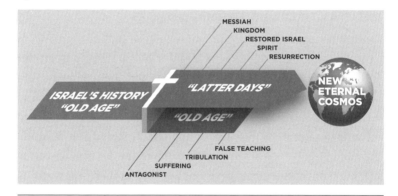

Figure 5.2

Though all facets of the latter days have begun to be fulfilled in Christ and the church, they have not reached their consummate state of fulfillment. The New Testament looks forward to the future when God will fully establish the kingdom (1 Corinthians 15:24), physically resurrect believers and unbelievers (John 5:28-29), and create the new heavens and earth (Revelation 21:1).

Understanding the already–not yet can be a bit tricky, so I'll attempt an illustration. One benefit of having a Sam's Club membership is their unrivaled food samples. From meat to sweet tea, Sam's Club provides daily samples to their customers. I find myself ignoring my shopping list and heading straight to their buffet of samples. The samples are just that—samples of the actual food. They are not analogous or cheap knockoffs; they are the real thing, only on a smaller scale. Perhaps the same could be said of inaugurated eschatology. Take, for example, the already–not yet of our resurrection. As Christians, we have already been raised with Christ on a spiritual level, but we await our full and final resurrection at Christ's second coming. Even our spiritual resurrection that takes place upon conversion is in part. We have a sample of what is to come. Our resurrection is indeed genuine, but it remains partial. We still have indwelling sin, and all of our thoughts and actions are tainted with sin. But when Christ returns we will experience a complete and thorough resurrection. In consequence, as we explore the New Testament's conception of Jesus as true Israel, the long-awaited king, we must do so with this endtime framework in mind.

JESUS AS TRUE AND FAITHFUL ISRAEL

The New Testament, especially the four Gospels, is quick to align Jesus of Nazareth with Adam and the nation of Israel. For the evangelists, Jesus' identity as the last Adam and true Israel is fundamental to their narratives. The connection between Jesus and Adam/Israel is stunningly woven into the fabric of each Gospel. One cannot fully understand the person of Jesus without appreciating the centrality of Adam's and Israel's story in the Gospels. Matthew 2:14-15 is a wonderful example of this reality. An angel appears to Joseph and commands him to go to Egypt, so that his family might remain safe. According to Matthew 2:15, it is precisely at this point when Hosea 11:1 is fulfilled: "So he [Joseph] got up, took the child and his mother during the night and left for Egypt, where he stayed until the death of Herod. And so was fulfilled what the Lord had said through the prophet: '*Out of Egypt I called my son.*'" Matthew claims that Hosea 11:1 was fulfilled in Jesus' journey to Egypt, even as a baby.

The immediate and broad context of Hosea 11 is critical to understanding Matthew's depiction of Jesus as true Israel. Hosea 11:1-4 recounts God's devotion to Israel by redeeming her out of Egypt (Hosea 11:1), but Israel did not remain faithful to him. Hosea 11:2 summarizes it well:

The more they were called,
the more they went away from me.

Hosea 11:1-4 highlights two ideas: the Lord's faithfulness to his covenant and Israel's unfaithfulness to that same covenant.

The book of Hosea, not unlike other prophetic books, oscillates between the one and the many, or "corporate solidarity." Often in the Old Testament, an individual corporately represents a community or even a nation. The actions of a single person affect the entire community. Saul's sin of killing the Gibeonites results in a famine in Israel (2 Samuel 21:1), and David's sin of numbering the people engenders punishment on Israel (1 Chronicles 21:1-17).

The same concept operates in Hosea. The prophet Hosea is commanded to "marry a promiscuous woman," so that Israel may see a graphic representation of their behavior. The symbolism between Hosea and Gomer is clear enough—Gomer represents unfaithful Israel and Hosea represents faithful Yahweh (Hosea 1:2). Hosea's children also represent Israel (Hosea 1:6, 8; cf. Hosea 12:2-5). Upon coming to Hosea 11:1 ("When Israel was a child, I loved him, and *out of Egypt I called my son*"), astute readers are keenly aware of the corporate solidarity that the prophet Hosea has already established.

The book of Hosea also predicts a time when a leader, one who represents the community, will lead them out of exile: "The people of Judah and the people of Israel will come together; *they will appoint one leader and will come up out of the land* [of Egypt]" (Hosea 1:11; cf. Hosea 7:11, 16; 8:13; 9:3; 11:5). Even within Hosea itself, there was an expectation that an individual would, in some way, trigger the restoration of Israel from exile in a second exodus.[1]

Making our way back to Matthew, the first Evangelist contrasts Israel as God's "son" in Hosea 11:1 with Jesus as the true "son" of God (Matthew 2:15). Keep in mind that the second exodus has already been in the forefront of Matthew's narrative well before his quotation of Hosea 11:1. Once Jesus, the sign child (Matthew 1:22-23), is born, magi come to worship him. Herod catches wind of this and orders that all the children under the age of two be killed (Matthew 2:1-18). Herod the Great, the Roman-appointed ruler

---

[1]G. K. Beale, "The Use of Hosea 11:1 in Matthew 2:15: One More Time," *JETS* 55 (2012): 697-715.

of Israel at this time, discovered that a rival king (Jesus) had been born
and attempted to kill this rival ruler (Matthew 2:1-18).

Like the wicked Pharaoh in Exodus 1:15–2:10, who unsuccessfully attempted
to murder all the male Israelite newborns, Herod, functioning as an anti-king
who oppresses God's people (Daniel 11:31), is unsuccessful in killing Jesus, the
greater Moses. The parallel between Moses and Jesus in the birth narrative
should not be forgotten. Pharaoh's attempt to kill Moses presages the latter Pharaoh's attempt to kill God's "firstborn," Israel (see Exodus 4:22). As the "firstborn
son" of God, the nation of Israel came out of Egypt, but they disobeyed and
incurred judgment. Jesus repeats the pattern by traveling out of Egypt, even as
a child (Matthew 2:14-23), yet he perfectly obeys his Father throughout his
ministry (see Matthew 3:15). Whereas Israel grumbled, complained, and lacked
faith in the Lord, Jesus perfectly obeyed the Father's will (Matthew 4:1-11).

Even before Jesus' public ministry began, Matthew identifies him as the
true, faithful Israel of God. The first Gospel readily connects Jesus' genealogy,
birth, journey to Egypt, baptism, and ministry to the nation of Israel. The
Old Testament recounts the failure of Adam and Israel in fulfilling the divine
requirements for imaging God on earth. God expected Adam and Israel to
rule on his behalf, worship him and mediate his presence to others, and obey
his law. But, as we've seen time and again, humanity is unable to obey perfectly.
So, the Old Testament looked forward to the very end of history, when God

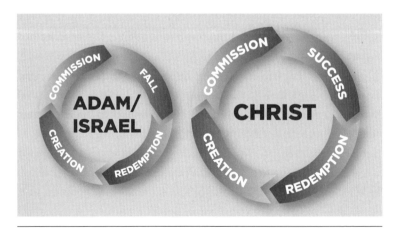

Figure 5.3

would raise up a faithful individual who would conquer Israel's enemies, bring God's glory to the ends of the earth, and obey his decrees. C. H. Dodd is on the right track when he argues, "The Messiah is not only founder and leader of the Israel-to-be, the new people of God; he is its 'inclusive representative.' In a real sense, he *is* the true Israel, carrying through in his own experience the process through which it comes into being"[2] (see fig. 5.3).

As we turn to the New Testament, we learn that Jesus of Nazareth is God's chosen one who has come to do what Adam and Israel failed to accomplish—succeed as a faithful king, priest, and prophet. Jesus inherits a mission, a mission that requires individuals to obey God perfectly, conquer the devil, and expand God's glorious presence to the ends of the earth.

When we read the Gospels, we must appreciate Christ's earthly ministry in its simplicity and in its complexity as heading toward this goal. The life of Christ is the culmination of the Old Testament. Every chapter, ever paragraph, and every verse in the four Gospels reaches back, in some sense, to the Old Testament while simultaneously never losing sight of the person of Christ.

JESUS AS KING

The remainder of this chapter will focus on the first dimension of Christ as the last Adam and true Israel—Christ as king. As the long-awaited king of Israel, Jesus fulfills the expectations of the Old Testament. But Jesus' reign differs from expectations. His rule is not marked by political triumph but by suffering and death. In the image of God, his kingship also far exceeds expectations in that he rules not over a territory in the Middle East but over the entire cosmos.

Jesus as the long-awaited king. We could summarize Matthew's Gospel in one word—fulfillment. From beginning to end, Matthew views Jesus' genealogy, birth, life, death, and resurrection as the fulfillment of the entire sweep of the Old Testament. For Matthew, all of the Old Testament—its institutions, significant events, and persons—anticipates Jesus of Nazareth. The Gospel of Matthew places Jesus squarely at the center of God's story of redemption. At the beginning of the first Gospel, Jesus is formally introduced as "the Messiah the Son of David, the Son of Abraham" (Matthew 1:1). By not following the

---

[2]C. H. Dodd, *The Founder of Christianity* (London: Macmillan, 1970), 106 (emphasis original).

chronological sequence of Israel's history (Abraham lived before David), Jesus' royal pedigree remains primary throughout Matthew's genealogy. Though some of the genealogy remains elusive to us, the overall point cannot be missed: Jesus is the long-awaited king of Israel. Israel and her prophets waited expectantly for hundreds of years for the Messiah's coming (see, e.g., Genesis 3:15; 49:8-10; 2 Samuel 7:12-13), and he has now arrived in the person of Jesus. Even the genealogy's structure expresses this messianic theme. The structure breaks down into three chronological sections: premonarchal period (Matthew 1:2-6a), monarchal period up to the exile (Matthew 1:6b-11), and the deportation to the long-awaited Messiah (Matthew 1:12-16). The arrangement of the genealogy displays a wonderful focus on Jesus as the end-time ruler of Israel.

Why also mention the great patriarch Abraham? Matthew does so for at least one salient reason: God promised Abraham that he would be the father of a great nation and that the nation would occupy the Promised Land (see, e.g., Genesis 12:1-9; 15:4-20). Jesus is the continuation and ultimate fulfillment of God's promise to Abraham in that he is a legitimate offspring of Abraham. He is *the* embodiment of what it means to be a descendant of Abraham, the true Israelite. To state the matter succinctly, Matthew presents the story of Jesus primarily through the lens of the end-time king and true Israel. Perhaps another reason why Abraham is mentioned stems from God's promise that "all peoples on earth / will be blessed through" him (Genesis 12:3). Jesus is the means by which God will restore his image in humanity, including among the Gentiles, just as the prophets anticipated (e.g., Isaiah 2:2; 61:11; Zechariah 14:16-19).

Learning about one's ancestry is big business these days. For a few dollars, I can go online and discover long-lost aunts and uncles and reconstruct my genealogy. While Matthew's genealogy does provide us with some historical insight, it is far more concerned with the narrative of redemption attached to each name. Each person Matthew includes, whether it's Asa or Shealtiel, is tied to a story, a story that may have seemed insignificant at the time but is actually part of God's glorious plan of redemption. God has worked through every person in the Old Testament to prepare the way for the coming Redeemer.

The baptism of Jesus. The baptism of Jesus in the Jordan River is a profoundly important event. It is here where Jesus begins his public ministry and sees himself as Adam and Israel. Jesus claims that his baptism will "fulfill all righteousness" (Matthew 3:15). Like the first generation of Israelites passing through the Red Sea and the second generation of Israelites wading through the Jordan River, Jesus graciously identifies with corrupt Israel. But where the first and second generations of the nation of Israel failed upon their passing through the water, Jesus succeeds in his temptation.

At the baptism, the Spirit descends on Jesus "like a dove" (Matthew 3:16 and par.). The presence of the Spirit alighting on Jesus triggers the fulfillment of several Old Testament passages that predict the descent of the Spirit at the very end of history, when Israel is redeemed (e.g., Ezekiel 37:4-14; Joel 2:1-32). Jesus is presented, in some sense, as experiencing a personal Pentecost (cf. Acts 1–2). Just as Adam received the breath or Spirit of God in Genesis 2:7 and Israel received the glory of God at Sinai, God pours out his Spirit in a more powerful and intimate way on his Son. Jesus is *the* faithful Adam, the true and perfect Israel (see fig. 5.4).

The redemption of God's people begins at Jesus' baptism in the Jordan. "Jesus' baptism, like his impending death . . . would be vicarious, embraced on behalf of others with whom the Father had called him to identify."[3] Israel's restoration is now at hand through the person of Jesus. As the long-awaited king (Matthew 3:17 and par.; 2 Samuel 7:14; Psalm 2:7), Jesus repeats the history of Israel to lead them out of spiritual exile and deliver them into the Promised Land of the new creation. Jesus' faithful career as a faithful King, climaxing in his death and resurrection, is *for* the benefit of others. What a marvelous truth it is that Christ came to humanity not "to be served, but to serve, and to give his life as a ransom for many" (Mark 10:45). He became a faithful King so that his followers could become faithful kings.

Mark's messianic secret. Within the Synoptics, especially Mark, Jesus insists that his disciples and others conceal his identity. Commentators have labeled this phenomenon the "messianic secret." For example, in Mark 1:34, Jesus exorcises demons but prohibits them from divulging his identity: "Jesus healed many who had various diseases. He also drove out many demons, but *he would not let the demons speak because they knew who he was.*" Again, we

---

[3]Craig S. Keener, *The Gospel of Matthew: A Socio-rhetorical Commentary* (Grand Rapids: Eerdmans, 2009), 132.

can make a similar observation in Mark 8:30, which immediately follows Peter's accurate confession that Jesus is indeed "the Christ" (i.e., the "Messiah"): "Jesus warned them *not to tell anyone about him*" (cf. Mark 9:9). Why does Jesus forbid his disciples from telling others his identity as Israel's long-awaited king? Doesn't Jesus want Israel to know that he's their Savior who has come to liberate them from political and spiritual oppression? The answer rests on Jesus' fulfillment of Israel's expectations of the long-awaited Messiah. For us to grasp the significance of the messianic secret, we must briefly survey a few key Old Testament texts that describe the coming Messiah.

Figure 5.4

We saw in the previous chapter that many Old Testament passages expect a coming king who will deliver Israel and redeem her from her plight. The Old Testament collectively speaks of an individual who is "anointed" for a specific purpose—ruling over Israel and the nations and redeeming all of creation. That the Messiah should suffer persecution in some capacity is also mentioned in a few passages. Daniel 9:25-26 seems to suggest that the Messiah (the "Anointed One" in the NIV) will eventually be put to death: "From the time the word goes out to restore and rebuild Jerusalem until the Anointed One, the ruler, comes, there will be seven 'sevens,' and sixty-two 'sevens.' . . . After the sixty-two 'sevens,' *the Anointed One will be put to death and will have nothing*" (cf. Isaiah 52:13–53:12; Zechariah 12:10).

We are now in a better position to answer why in Mark's Gospel Jesus commanded individuals to stay quiet. Answer: Jesus must alter and refocus their understanding of the Messiah (and the kingdom he establishes). The end-time kingdom and Jesus' kingship are marked first not by political, earthly, physical triumph but by suffering and death.

Before heading south to Jerusalem where he would eventually be crucified, Jesus asks his disciples about his identity: "Who do people say I am?" (Mark 8:27). After the disciples offer their list of prime candidates, Jesus pointedly asks Peter, "Who do you say I am?" The bell rings, and Peter hits the nail on the head when he declares, "You are the *Messiah*" (Mark 8:29). The word here for "Messiah" is the Greek term *christos*, meaning "anointed one" or "Christ." Peter claims that Jesus is indeed the highly anticipated Messiah who has come to liberate Israel. But Jesus' messiahship breaks the mold, as he is a *suffering* Messiah who ushers in a kingdom marked by persecution and suffering (Mark 8:31–9:1).

Jesus indeed fulfills the Old Testament expectations that prophesied the Messiah's suffering and death as well as his triumph. But the way in which the Old Testament is fulfilled in the person of Jesus is different from expectations. The disciples will only be able to grasp this truth after the crucifixion and the resurrection. Only then will they understand the true and complete nature of Jesus' identity and the kingdom he establishes.

In some sense, Jesus' messiahship embodies the overlap of the ages—the arrival of the kingdom and the presence of the end-time tribulation—during his earthly ministry and on the cross. He is king during his ministry of weakness, especially at the moment of suffering and death. The three Synoptics encourage the reader to connect the dots by showing them how the fate of the Messiah is bound up with that of the kingdom. John, on the other hand, is far more explicit in this regard. In John's Gospel, the theme of being "lifted up" is a double entendre—it refers physically to the lifting up of Jesus on the cross and figuratively to his exaltation or "lifting up" (John 3:14; 8:28; 12:32). While Jesus is suffering a shameful death on the cross, he is ironically the supreme ruler. Seyoon Kim agrees: "The cross is the ground of boasting for the Christian because it is the cross of the Lord . . . who has triumphed over the world and its rulers precisely on that cross. . . . The cross which is a sign of defeat and shame, foolishness and scandal for those who are perishing in the world, is a sign of triumph and boasting, wisdom and glory for those who are called."[4]

Though a suffering Messiah was to some degree anticipated, messianic suffering does not play a central role in the Old Testament. The vast majority of first-century Jews did not expect that the Messiah would be crucified, much less be seen as a glorious divine ruler actually exercising ruling power while being defeated. This understanding of the Messiah develops Old Testament and Jewish expectations. People rejected Christ because he didn't fit their version of what a redeemer should be. Even today, many reject Christianity because the cross turns the world's firm convictions on their head. The cross embraces shame, humility, defeat, and death, whereas it shuns every attempt of human boasting. God prizes what humanity degrades.

As the perfect image of God, Jesus ironically rules over Israel's enemies by being physically conquered. He is, as the book of Revelation states, simultaneously the "Lion of the tribe of Judah" and a "Lamb, looking as if it had been slain" (Revelation 5:5-6). While Jesus is suffering a shameful death on the cross, he is simultaneously the supreme messianic ruler. Note how two separate strands are now fused in Christ. Jesus, as the last Adam, must suffer

---

[4]Seyoon Kim, *The Origin of Paul's Gospel*, WUNT 4 (Tübingen: Mohr Siebeck, 1981; repr., Grand Rapids: Eerdmans, 1981), 80-81.

for the sin of the first Adam. But in his suffering, Jesus rules over the serpent—an act that the first Adam was to accomplish before the fall. So Jesus begins to restore the divine image in humanity by bearing the penalty that he did not deserve. Jesus genuinely fulfills the divine commission to Adam to subdue his enemies in Genesis 1:28 by himself being subdued by the Jewish authorities, the Romans, and the devil. God's original intention for humanity to rule over the created order is now genuinely taking place in the person of Jesus.

The firstborn of creation. Without hesitation, the Gospels insist that Jesus is the long-awaited king of Israel. Yet, as we've seen, his rule differs from expectations. He rules in the midst of suffering and weakness. Another dimension of Jesus' rule that differs from, even exceeds, expectations is his cosmic rule as the Lord of Israel. The apostle Paul's hymn in Colossians 1:15-20 addresses two dimensions of Christ being in the "image" of God: (1) the chronological priority of Christ (his preexistence)—Christ's supremacy over the first creation (Colossians 1:15-17); and (2) the creational priority of Christ—his supremacy over the new creation (Colossians 1:18-20).[5]

Within the first portion of the hymn (Colossians 1:15-18a), Christ is viewed as the preincarnate Adam, after whom the first Adam was patterned. Perhaps it seems strange to consider that even before Christ became human, his preexistent state should be understood as being in the "image of God." So when Christ is incarnated and becomes human, his identity as the last Adam is rooted in and flows from his preexistent state.[6] In other words, Christ was in the image of God in his eternal state before his incarnation, and that existence is the model for humanity being in the image of God. This explains Paul's allusion in Colossians 1:15 to Genesis 1:27:

> God created mankind *in his own image,*
> > in *the image of God* he created them;
> > male and female He created them. (cf. 1 Corinthians 11:7;
> > > 2 Corinthians 4:4)

---

[5]G. K. Beale, "Colossians," in *Commentary on the New Testament Use of the Old Testament,* ed. G. K. Beale and D. A. Carson (Grand Rapids: Baker Academic, 2007), 851.

[6]Lane G. Tipton, "Christology in Colossians 1:15-20 and Hebrews 1:1-4: An Exercise in Biblico-systematic Theology," in *Resurrection and Eschatology: Essays in Honor of Richard B. Gaffin, Jr.,* ed. Lane G. Tipton and Jeffrey C. Waddington (Phillipsburg, NJ: P&R, 2008).

Paul has taken the language of the first Adam and used it to describe the preincarnate Christ. Simply put, God fashioned the first Adam in the garden after the preincarnate Christ.

Sonship is intimately tethered to bearing one's image. God's relationship to Adam illustrates this relationship. Since Adam is created in God's image, he is deemed to be God's "son." Adam's son Seth was said to be in Adam's image: "When Adam had lived 130 years, he had a *son* in his own likeness, *in his own image*; and he named him Seth" (Genesis 5:3). The first Adam, being in the image of God, was to rule over the created order on behalf of God. But, as we know all too well, Adam failed. So God raised up others and made them "in his image" (Seth, Noah, Abraham, Isaac, etc.). They were fashioned to rule over the created order and spread God's glorious presence. Finally, God sent his own Son to earth, who was also in his pristine image. But in Colossians 1:15 Christ's preincarnate divine rule is in focus. Jesus is God's divine Son, which means that he is also in the image of his Father (Colossians 1:13).

Paul also calls Christ "the firstborn": "The Son is the image of the invisible God, *the firstborn* over all creation" (Colossians 1:15). Though some argue that Christ being the firstborn reflects a creaturely state, this is both theologically and exegetically problematic (cf. John 1:3). Christ's status as the "firstborn" is not to be taken as a literal depiction (i.e., Christ is literally the first one born) but a figurative expression. This particular concept is rooted in the Old Testament:[7] "Then say to Pharaoh, 'This is what the LORD says: Israel is my *firstborn* son'" (Exodus 4:22; cf. Psalm 89:27; Hebrews 1:6). These texts do not refer to a literal or physical firstborn but to relational priority. Christ is the firstborn because he is the most supreme being (not because he is created). The prophesied messianic king in Psalm 89:27 is "firstborn" because he is the supreme sovereign over all. Paul's point in Colossians 1:15 is quite clear—Christ is preexistent and sovereign over the created order.

The second portion of the hymn is stunningly majestic and focused on Christ (Colossians 1:18b-20). It centers on how Christ relates to the new order of creation. Christ, as a resurrected being, has begun the end-time renewal

---

[7]Craig S. Keener, *The IVP Bible Background Commentary: New Testament*, 2nd ed. (Downers Grove, IL: IVP Academic, 2014), 571.

of the cosmos ("and through him to reconcile to himself all things" [Colossians 1:20]). "The Creator has imaged himself in the creation, all the while warning against humans taking any part of creation as the final image of the Creator. When the Creator stepped into creation, a new creation was effected."[8]

Christ also embodies God's glorious presence, as the end-time temple. This is the same divine presence that was partially housed in Israel's mobile tabernacle and in the temple. Now in the new age God's unfettered presence has descended to earth in Christ (cf. Matthew 1:22-23). The expectation that heaven and earth would be joined together in Genesis 1–2 is finally being realized.

The Old Testament prophesies that a coming Messiah would usher in God's eternal kingdom in the latter days by vanquishing Israel's enemies (e.g., Genesis 49; Numbers 24). But does the Old Testament anticipate that the end-time Messiah would be a divine, preexistent being? The Old Testament contains a few texts that may suggest some inkling of messianic preexistence and thus messianic deity (e.g., Exodus 3:2; Isaiah 9:6; Dan 7:13-14; Micah 5:2).

The New Testament often attributes acts and characteristics to Christ that only God performs and possesses. It is also not a matter of coincidence that the New Testament ascribes sovereign rule and creational authority to Christ (e.g., John 1:1-5; Colossians 1:15-20; Hebrews 1:2-4). By and large, the New Testament connects Jesus' life, mission, and identity with that of Israel's God in the Old Testament.

Nevertheless, we must readily admit that the Old Testament did not develop the idea of the arrival of a divine, preexistent Messiah to a great extent. That is, the Old Testament did not clearly identify the Messiah's being or actions with that of the Lord. We are given a faint yet legitimate expectation of this particular aspect. Unlike the latter-day Messiah's prerogative to rule, his preexistence is not developed in much detail; we only have a few texts that point in this direction. Perhaps we could put these texts on a trajectory of sorts, the end of which is a full-blown development of the doctrine of preexistence and deity of the Messiah as seen in the New Testament.

---

[8]Richard Lints, *Identity and Idolatry: The Image of God and Its Inversion*, NSBT 36 (Downers Grove, IL: IVP Academic, 2015), 122.

CONCLUSIONS AND APPLICATION

If there's one word that summarizes this chapter it's this: *success*. Where the Old Testament recounts the failure of Adam and Israel, the four Gospels narrate the success of Jesus as the last Adam and true Israel. One of the more remarkable facets of the Old Testament is its unvarnished narratives. The great patriarchs of Israel, for example, are portrayed as righteous but deeply flawed individuals. Abraham lied, David committed adultery and murder, King Solomon worshiped false gods, and the list goes on and on. The writers of the Old Testament longed for the day when a faithful individual would arrive and make right what had gone wrong.

The New Testament also identifies Christ with the God of the Old Testament. He reigns and creates as Israel's Lord. But what does Christ's deity have to do with being in the divine image and successfully ruling over God's enemies? Jesus is fully God and fully human. He is the God of Israel and the last Adam and true Israel. God commanded Adam and Israel to rule over their environment, subdue rebellion, and bring order out of chaos. Yet both failed to accomplish the divine mandate. God took it on himself to fulfill the demands that he himself stipulated. Jesus is God's divine Son, which means that he is also in the image of his Father (Colossians 1:13). Christ's rule is not confined to a plot of land but extends to the far corners of the cosmos. Through his death and resurrection, Jesus' rule even exceeds what was expected of Adam, since he rules over the entire created order, including the invisible realm. Christ doesn't rule the cosmos on behalf of God. He rules as God!

One central reason why the church assembles on Sunday is to celebrate Christ's enthronement as cosmic king. Revelation 5:13-14 reads,

> Then I heard every creature in heaven and on earth and under the earth and on the sea, and all that is in them, saying:
>
> "To him who sits on the throne and to the Lamb
>   be praise and honor and glory and power,
> for ever and ever!"
>
> The four living creatures said, "Amen," and the elders fell down and worshiped.

May the praise of heaven echo in our hearts on earth.

RECOMMENDED READING

Johnson, Dennis E. *Walking with Jesus Through His Word*. Phillipsburg, NJ: P&R, 2015.

Ladd, George Eldon. *The Presence of the Future*. Rev. ed. Grand Rapids: Eerdmans, 2000.

Schreiner, Thomas R. *The King in His Beauty: A Biblical Theology of the Old and New Testaments*. Grand Rapids: Baker Academic, 2013.

Thompson, Alan J. *The Acts of the Risen Lord: Luke's Account of God's Unfolding Plan*. Downers Grove, IL: IVP Academic, 2011.

Wright, N. T. *Jesus and the Victory of God*. Christian Origins and the Question of God 2. Minneapolis: Fortress, 1996.

Chapter Six

JESUS AS PRIEST

AS PRIESTS, ADAM AND EVE were to minister in God's garden sanctuary in Eden and expand God's glory to the ends of the earth. But they failed in that they allowed the serpent to invade the sanctuary of Eden, failed to remove all unclean things from God's presence, and failed to expand the paradise of Eden. So too the nation of Israel was to eradicate all forms of sin and filth from their community and mediate God's presence to the surrounding nations. Yet they failed to live out God's intention for the nation as a "kingdom of priests" (Exodus 19:6). The New Testament highlights Jesus' ministry as a faithful priest in expelling wickedness and rebellion from the created order and bringing God's glory to the nations.

The four Evangelists pay careful attention to Jesus' interaction with the temple in Jerusalem. Fundamental to Jesus' mission is his fulfillment of the Old Testament's expectation that God would one day dwell intimately with humanity and creation. The sanctuaries in Eden and Sinai, as well as the mobile tabernacle and Solomon's temple, pointed forward to this end-time reality. I mentioned previously that the temple comprised three parts, each section corresponding to a cosmic reality: the outer courts symbolized the earth, the holy place signified the visible heavens, and the holy of holies represented the invisible heavens were God dwells with his angels. The symbolism of the temple indicates that God's presence will, at the very end of history, eventually break out from the heavenly holy of holies and fill every parcel of the new cosmos.

Originally constructed by Solomon, then rebuilt by Zerubbabel and refurbished by Herod, the temple was Israel's pride and joy. Growing up just miles from Washington, DC, I often marveled at the capital city's architecture, museums, cemeteries, and landscape. Millions of people visit the capital each year and take in the sights and sounds of our nation's seat of government. Like Washington, DC, the Jerusalem temple was the centerpiece of the nation of Israel. It's what set apart the nation from the foreign nations. In Luke 21:5 the disciples gleefully point out to Jesus "how the temple was adorned with beautiful stones and with gifts dedicated to God." On a physical level, Israel's temple was beautiful and awe-inspiring, but on a deeper level the temple reeked of spiritual grime and filth.

The New Testament depicts Jesus' relationship to the Jerusalem temple primarily in two ways: (1) Since Jesus has ushered in the new age and God's presence is among his people, there is no need for the physical temple. Jesus is now the true temple, and God's glory has descended in a unique way in the person of Christ. (2) The temple itself has become a place of rampant idolatry, so the time has come for God to judge the temple. Jesus simultaneously fulfills the Old Testament expectation that God would dwell with humanity and, as a faithful priest, purges evil from Israel's temple. We will now examine both of these dimensions in turn.

JESUS AS THE END-TIME TEMPLE

John's prologue explicitly connects the person of Christ with Israel's tabernacle: "The Word became flesh and *made his dwelling among us*. We have seen his glory, *the glory of the one and only Son*, who came from the Father, full of grace and truth" (John 1:14). The term translated "made his dwelling" is peculiar and could be rendered as "tabernacled," a term that recalls the wilderness wanderings. When Israel left Sinai, God commanded Israel to build the mobile tabernacle in order that his glorious presence would continue to "dwell among them" during their wilderness wanderings (Exodus 25:8). As the glory of God filled Israel's tabernacle (Exodus 40:34-35), so too the glory of God tabernacles in Jesus. The presence of God, formerly contained in the holy of holies, has begun to fill the earth in Jesus—Israel's Lord incarnate. Heaven has come down! First Peter 2:4 states that Christ is the "living Stone" of the end-time temple. Christ is a "living Stone" because he is the true temple. The physical temple was never intended to be an end in itself; rather, it was a temporary residence that partially housed God's glory, a symbol of something (and someone) greater to come. King Solomon, at the dedication of Israel's temple, even admitted as much: "But will God really dwell on earth? The heavens, even the highest heaven, cannot contain you. How much less this temple I have built!" (1 Kings 8:27; cf. Isaiah 66:1; Acts 7:48-49). So, as the living Stone, Christ is the true temple of God and the fullest expression of God's glory on earth. Peter then goes to on argue that all those who are united to Christ are "living stones . . . being built into a spiritual house" (1 Peter 2:5). The same glory that was in Eden with Adam and Eve and in the Jerusalem temple now dwells more fully in believers on account of their identification with Christ.

As priests, Adam and the nation of Israel were to mediate God's presence to the farthest corners of the earth. Now that Christ has come, that expectation has become a reality. Jesus of Nazareth is the means by which God's glory is spreading throughout the earth. But Jesus is more than a mediator of God's presence. He is God. Despite being created in God's image, perfected humanity was designed to be enraptured in God's glory, to dwell with God in his fullness in the new creation. Yet Scripture draws a clear line between humanity and God. God's glory is unique to the triune God and is not endemic to us. In this respect, Christ's priestly office exceeds expectations. Just as the Old Testament did not develop in detail the idea of a divine Messiah, so too the Old Testament did not develop the idea that the Messiah would be *the* end-time temple. Certainly, prominent Old Testament figures played a significant role in the establishment of sacred space (Adam, Solomon, etc.), but God's unique and glorious presence never fully dwelt in these figures like it does in the person of Christ.[1]

---

[1]See the discussion in G. K. Beale and Benjamin L. Gladd, *Hidden but Now Revealed: A Biblical Theology of Mystery* (Downers Grove, IL: IVP Academic, 2014), 293-95.

THE TEMPLE "CLEANSING"

As the perfect priest, Christ begins to expel all forms of idolatry and rebellion that contaminated the created order. The four Gospels include accounts of Jesus ridding the temple of Jerusalem of idolatry. The Synoptics place the event at the beginning of passion week (Matthew 21:12-13; Mark 11:15-17; Luke 19:45-46), whereas John narrates the event at the beginning of Jesus' ministry (John 2:13-25). Though it's not clear if Jesus "cleansed" the temple once or twice during his career, as a good case can be made for both, we can be confident that the event is critical to each Gospel.

Instead of being a place to worship the Lord and welcome the Gentile nations (Mark 11:17), the temple in Jerusalem had become a bastion of pride and financial gain for the nation. God's original intention was for his presence to go forth to all the nations, not to be hoarded and scandalized. As a result, Jesus drives out the moneychangers from the courtyard and "would not allow anyone to carry merchandise through the temple courts" (Mark 11:16). By forbidding the sale of sacrifices that offer ritual cleansing to the Israelites, Jesus is denouncing the basic function of the Jerusalem temple—to house the glory of God. Jesus goes on to quote Isaiah 56:7, a prophecy that the temple would become a rallying point for the nations (Isaiah 56:3-8). Ironically, the temple, a house intended to bless all the nations, was used to prevent the nations from worship.

I have argued throughout this study that unbelievers retain God's image, albeit in a perverted state. The fall marred God's image in all of humanity, and all of Adam and Eve's descendants abuse the divine image. The kingly, priestly, and prophetic aspects of God's image are now instruments for destruction and self-exaltation. Instead of magnifying God throughout the earth, unbelievers magnify themselves. The Genesis 1:28 commission is turned on its head. One key reason why Jesus judges the temple is his desire to rid the earth of sin's filth. The Jewish leaders, representing the nation, are anti-priests. Instead of obeying God's law and keeping the nation and her temple free from defilement, the Jewish leaders promoted greed and lust for power, defiling God's people and her sanctuary. Instead of mediating God's presence to the nations, the Jewish leaders cordoned off the temple from the Gentiles.

A well-known inscription, part of the original balustrade, separated Gentile proselytes from the ethnic Jews. It reads, "No man of another nation is to enter within the barrier and enclosure around the temple. Whoever is caught will have himself to blame for his death which follows."[2] The point is that God-fearing Gentiles, though they converted to Judaism, were treated as second-class citizens. The irony here is of the highest order—the Jewish leaders, in an attempt to preserve the sanctity of the temple, kept Gentiles at arm's length from the temple. In so doing, they ended up defiling the very place they were to intent on protecting!

How often do we commit this same sin? Do we only fellowship with people who are like us? Do we only invite people to church who look like us and are of the same social standing? The community of saints is intended to be composed of people "from every nation, tribe, people and language" (Revelation 7:9). How tempting it is to indict the Jewish leaders of failing to be concerned about the nations and all the while we are doing the same in our neighborhoods and communities.

In judging Israel's physical temple, Jesus clears the way for the establishment of the end-time temple, where outcasts gather and enjoy God's presence (Isaiah 56:3-8). Instead of dwelling partially in a building, God's glory has descended in his Son, and those who join themselves to Jesus become part of this latter-day temple, regardless of their ethnicity.

Jesus is concerned not only with an idolatrous temple but also with the entire created order. Since the temple in Jerusalem symbolizes the cosmos, it may not be a stretch to view Jesus' actions in the temple as indicative of his larger, cosmic agenda—the eradication of all forms of evil in the cosmos. When Jesus heals the blind, the lame, and the mute, he signals the in-breaking of the new creation and the extermination of sin's desecration. The restored people of God are spiritually and physically whole, as they are part of the new creation, fit for the new heavens and earth.

Though these healings were not physically permanent, they were symbolic expressions of the in-breaking kingdom of the new creation and pointed to consummate physical healing in the eternal, new creation. The same could

---

[2]Everett Ferguson, *Backgrounds of Early Christianity*, 3rd. ed. (Grand Rapids: Eerdmans, 2003), 562.

be said of the Synoptics' emphasis on Jesus' victory over the spiritual realm. After Jesus initially defeats the devil, the captain of the antagonistic forces of evil, in the wilderness temptation, he systematically begins to overthrow the demons who have long enslaved humanity. A cardinal aspect of Jesus' mission in his priestly office is therefore the eradication of the effects of the fall on the entire created order. For God to dwell with humanity and creation, all unclean things must be eliminated. Recall that one of the reasons why God created Adam in his image is so that he would "work" and "take care" of the garden (Genesis 2:15). The first couple failed in their responsibility in keeping the sacred space of Eden clean from defilement, whereas Jesus fulfilled Genesis 2:15 and began to purge the cosmos of sin.

All believers are perfectly righteous and holy in God's sight on account of Christ's work, yet sin remains and must be purged. As I reflect on my own life, I think about how on the weekends, I enjoy cleaning cars with my two boys. For some reason, I'm obsessed with clean windshields, and it's not uncommon for me to wipe them clean four or five times a week. There's nothing worse than driving with a dirty windshield! I am a fanatic about wiping away dirty spots and bits of dust. If only I had the same passion to clean my heart of sin by seeking forgiveness from God and took the right precautions for preventing sinful habits. Our right standing before God (justification) should and will propel us to rid our hearts of sin through his grace (sanctification).

A BETTER PRIEST AND SACRIFICE

As we've seen, the Old Testament presents the Garden of Eden as the first sanctuary, wherein Adam and Eve dwelt with the Lord. Genesis 3 narrates the fall of Adam and Eve, which results in their exile and banishment from God's glory. Stained with guilt and sin, a sacrifice was needed to make reparations. So apparently an animal sacrifice was offered to God as Adam and Eve were given "garments of skin" (Genesis 3:21). A holy God cannot tolerate any form of sin.

The Old Testament regulates many different forms of offerings and sacrifices, and central to these rituals is God's presence among his people. The book of Leviticus outlines the way in which a righteous and holy God can dwell with sinful individuals in the tabernacle. Leviticus 9 sets forth the sacrificial rituals in the following order: expiation (burnt offerings), consecration (grain offerings), and fellowship with God (peace offerings). Once the peace offering had been made, "the glory of the LORD appeared to all the people" (Leviticus 9:23). The climax of the temple cult was the Day of Atonement, when the high priest entered the holy of holies once a year and sprinkled blood on the mercy seat (Leviticus 16). Sin had to be dealt with before the worshiper could enjoy fellowship with the Lord.

The one key purpose of the temple rituals was to remove sinful contaminants that defile the worshiper—like the removal of dirt and grime from a window. Even before Moses outlined the various rituals that Israel was to perform, as described in the books of Exodus and Leviticus, the Old Testament often narrates prominent individuals presenting sacrifices to the Lord (e.g., Genesis 4:4; 8:20-21; 12:6-8; 22:2-13). For Israel to enjoy the glory of her Lord, atonement for sin needed to be made. God's wrath had to be appeased. But a few problems quickly surfaced as the Old Testament unfolded: sacrifices are unable to atone fully for sin (see Hosea 6:6), and Israel and her priests were incapable of faithfully offering up sacrifices (e.g., 1 Samuel 15:21-22). The book of Isaiah understands these deficiencies and predicts that a future "servant" figure will become "an offering for sin" and will "justify many" within Israel (Isaiah 53:10-11). For complete atonement to be made, a faithful and righteous individual will offer himself up as the ultimate sacrifice in the latter days. An animal simply will not do.

The New Testament is quick to point out that Jesus is the ultimate sacrifice, whose death atones for sin. The time has come for God to deal once and for all with sin. John the Baptist without hesitation declared that Jesus was the "Lamb of God, who takes away the sin of the world" (John 1:29). God's end-time wrath was appeased in his Son's death, resulting in reconciliation between God and humanity. Christ's death and resurrection paved the way for God to dwell with believers. But Jesus is not only the perfect sacrifice, he is also the perfect high priest. Where the Old Testament tends to separate these two realities, the New Testament joins them. Christ is both sacrifice and high priest (Hebrews 7:27; 9:12). He offered up himself!

As the faithful priest, Jesus is intent on creating a holy people out of a defiled people. But in order for God's people to be perfectly devoted to the Lord, Jesus himself must be defiled. His defilement leads to our holiness. What's remarkable here is that God is passionate about restoring his divine image imprinted on humanity. He's so passionate that he even sent his holy Son to be unholy in our stead. Jesus' office of priest is brilliantly on display as he hangs on the cross and offers himself up for his people. The result of Christ's work on the cross brings us right back to God's intention in the Garden of Eden. He desired to dwell intimately with humanity, who bear his image, and now, as a result of Christ's work, that intention is finally realized.

TO THE ENDS OF THE EARTH

The final dimension to Jesus' priestly mission is his fulfillment of the original commission of Genesis 1:28. God commanded Adam and Eve to expand the Garden of Eden: "Be fruitful and increase in number; fill the earth and subdue it." Since God's presence was confined to the garden, as Eden expands, so does God's glory. The same could be said for the nation of Israel. The nation was to mediate God's presence to the surrounding nations. But both parties failed to bring God's glory to the farthest corners of the earth. Jesus' ministry, however, gets the ball rolling, and God's glorious presence begins to burst forth on the earth. The same presence that was limited to the holy of holies is now dwelling in Christ. The veil in the temple has torn, and God's presence is now filling the earth in that all who trust Christ enjoy God's glory in a profound and intimate manner.

Matthew 28:16-20, often labeled the Great Commission, is very much a part of the original commission of Genesis 1:28. Like the appointing of the twelve disciples, the Great Commission takes place on a mountain, once again signaling to the reader that God has come down in Jesus of Nazareth. The glorious presence that dwelt with Adam in the garden and with Israel at Sinai is now with the disciples but in a greater way. Christ is a fuller manifestation of God's glory, as he is truly "God with us" (Matthew 1:22-23 / Isaiah 7:14).

Jesus claims that "all authority in heaven and on earth has been given to me" (Matthew 28:18). This well-known statement fulfills Daniel 7:13-14, a prophecy about "one like a son of man" receiving "authority, glory and

sovereign power" forever. As the Son of Man, Jesus charges the disciples
with the Great Commission: "Go and make disciples of all nations . . .
teaching them . . . and surely I am with you always" (Matthew 28:19-20).
The Genesis 1:28 commission to Adam hangs in the background of this
pronouncement. Now that the disciples enjoy a restored image of God, they
are tasked with bringing others into the kingdom, so that the nations can
also experience a restored image. Since Jesus will go with the disciples,
success is guaranteed.

Recall our previous discussion of Daniel 7 and its prediction that a future
king, the Son of Man, will rule over all the hostile kingdoms at the very end
of history (Daniel 7:13-14). Daniel 7 presents the Son of Man as an Adam
figure who has successfully ruled over God's enemies. The language of "man,"
"beasts," "rule," and "kingdom" recalls Genesis 1–3. But where the first Adam
failed to rule over the serpent, the Son of Man rules over the beasts. The
Son of Man inherits what the first Adam should have inherited. The result
of the Son of Man's success is the eternal kingdom. We also learned that in
the second half of Daniel 7, the righteous remnant of Israel will "receive
the kingdom and will possess it forever" (Daniel 7:18; see Daniel 7:22, 27).
The Son of Man and the righteous Israelites are to be identified with one
another. The second portion of the vision identifies the Son of Man as the
"holy people" of Israel. According to Daniel 7, the triumphant saints have
finally appropriated that same rule over God's enemies through the victory
of the Son of Man.

As a result of the resurrection, Christ now rules over two realms—"heaven
and earth" (Matthew 28:18).[3] In his ministry, he possessed authority "on the
earth" by fulfilling the law, being the "Lord of the Sabbath" (Matthew 12:8),
forgiving sins, and so on. But when Jesus conquered Satan on the cross and
rose again, he gained possession of another territory—the heavenly realm.
Where the Gospels assume Christ's enthronement as cosmic King at the resurrection, Revelation makes it explicit. The entirety of Revelation 4–5 speaks
to this important issue, and Revelation 3:21 summarizes this event quite
nicely: "I [Christ] was victorious and sat down with my Father on his throne."

---

[3]Jonathan T. Pennington, *Heaven and Earth in the Gospel of Matthew*, NovTSup 126 (Leiden: Brill,
2007; repr. Grand Rapids: Baker, 2009), 205.

Christ rules from the very throne of God, a prerogative that only God possesses. This line of thinking fits quite well here in Matthew 28, where Jesus, as the triumphant Son of Man, empowers his disciples, the "holy people," to rule with him in subduing the nations and bringing them into the kingdom. Christ's cosmic rule now extends *through* the restored images of the disciples. They are imaging his rule on the earth.

As a faithful priest, Jesus promises to go with the disciples. Where they go, he goes. In chapter one we learned that the earth is composed of three levels of sanctity: Eden, the garden, and the outer world. Eden is the center of God's activity on the earth, where God dwelled with Adam and Eve. The farther Adam and Eve journeyed from Eden, the farther they traveled away from God's presence. The environment gradually became less and less holy. The first couple was responsible for transplanting Eden throughout the entire earth, so that it would be one gigantic temple, wherein God and humanity enjoyed perfect fellowship with one another.

It is fitting, then, that the Great Commission of Matthew 28 takes place on a mountain. The presence of Christ, as mediated by the Spirit (Acts 1:8), empowers the disciples to do what Adam and Israel failed to accomplish—mediate God's presence to those regions of the earth that are less holy. This mountain is ground zero, a spiritual Eden of sorts. The disciples must descend the mountain and bring God's glory to the nations. It will not be easy for the Eleven, as most of their fellow Jews will reject them. In the face of grave danger and opposition, though, Christ will "bless" and "shine on" the disciples (Numbers 6:24-25), spiritually nourishing and protecting his people with his presence. The net result of the Great Commission is the glory of God pervading every crevice of the earth. Mission accomplished.

CONCLUSION AND APPLICATION

In this chapter we looked at two areas of Jesus' identity as an end-time priest. We learned that Jesus is the ultimate fulfillment of Israel's temple. The sanctuary of Eden, Sinai, the mobile tabernacle, and Solomon's temple all prophetically anticipated his arrival. These previous dwelling places were incomplete, and God's full presence remained in heaven. But with the coming of Christ, God's full presence came down. God did indeed dwell intimately with Adam and Eve in Eden, but that experience paled in comparison to the disciples' encounter with Jesus.

As the true temple of God, Christ was on a mission to rid the cosmos of sin and fill it with God's glory. In the wilderness temptation and at the cross and resurrection, Christ dealt with sin in a definitive manner and decisively broke the devil's grasp on the created order. This is God's cosmos, and he intends on dwelling in it. Christ's role as priest is often neglected in our local churches. We talk of his kingship and sovereign power, but how often do we consider him as the true dwelling place of God? Do we contemplate Jesus as the ultimate mediator between God and humanity?

RECOMMENDED READING

Fletcher-Louis, C. "Priests and Priesthood." In *Dictionary of Jesus and the Gospels*, edited by Joel B. Green, 696-705. 2nd ed. Downers Grove, IL: IVP Academic.

Hamilton, James M., Jr. *With the Clouds of Heaven: The Book of Daniel in Biblical Theology*. NSBT 32. Downers Grove, IL: IVP Academic, 2014.

Heil, J. P. "Jesus as the Unique High Priest." *CBQ* 57 (1995): 729-55.

Perrin, Nicholas. *Jesus the Priest*. London: SPCK, 2018.

Stein, Robert H. *Jesus, the Temple and the Coming Son of Man: A Commentary on Mark 13*. Downers Grove, IL: IVP Academic, 2014.

Chapter Seven

JESUS AS PROPHET

A PROPHET IS SOMEONE who hears God's voice, speaks on his behalf, and embodies divine truth. I argued early on that Adam and Eve were to model their lives in accordance with God's law and teach his decrees to their descendants. The failure of Adam, the patriarchs, and Israel to obey God's law paved the way for Christ's success. As the obedient prophet, Jesus adheres to the law of God at every point. Yet Jesus is also portrayed as speaking as God himself. He's not only the voice of God on earth, he is God! The present chapter rounds out the discussion of Christ as a king, priest, and prophet, and it also serves as a bridge to the final four chapters.

THE WILDERNESS TEMPTATION

Christ's fulfillment of the office of a faithful prophet is wonderfully illustrated in his wilderness temptation. Over the forty-day testing in the Judean wilderness, Jesus obeys God's law and passes the test. This testing is the same grueling test that Adam experienced in the garden and Israel faced in the wilderness. The wilderness temptation in the Synoptics is critical to all three narratives. The basic plot is retained in all three: Jesus is baptized as Israel's king in the Jordan River and then successfully defeats the devil in the wilderness.

While all three Synoptics include the temptation narrative, only Luke and Matthew develop the event in some detail. In Mark and Matthew, the wilderness temptation immediately follows the baptism, whereas in Luke this event is included after the genealogy. Luke also uniquely traces Jesus' genealogy all the way back to Seth and Adam:

> . . . the son of Enosh,
> the son of *Seth*, the son of *Adam*,
> the son of God. (Luke 3:38)

Luke here refers the reader back to Genesis 5:1-3, a profoundly important text for understanding the image of God.

I have surmised that Genesis 5:1-3 traces the impartation of God's image. Just as God imparted his image to Adam, so also Adam imparts his image to Seth. Genesis 5:1-3 is intended to be read in light of Genesis 1:26-28 as a continuation or fulfillment, implying that Adam's descendants have begun to "rule" and "subdue" the earth. Though postfall humanity is in a state of rebellion, the chain has been broken. God graciously begins to restore his image and preserve a godly line through Seth and his descendants. By alluding to Genesis 5:1-3, Luke suggests that Jesus is a greater Adam, who bears the unblemished image of God. Jesus will begin to fulfill the Genesis 1:28 commission in his wilderness temptation.

Each Synoptic Evangelist claims that Jesus was tempted over a period of forty days (Matthew 4:2; Mark 1:13; Luke 4:1-2). It's easy to miss the rich background of Jesus' temptation, and perhaps some view Jesus' forty-day fast as evidence for an ancient food diet with great health benefits! But the qualification that this occurred in the wilderness, together with it being forty days, recalls Israel's temptation in the wilderness. Jesus' forty-day wilderness experience is a microcosm of Israel's forty-year experience of wandering in the desert.

As Jesus is led "by the Spirit into the wilderness" (Luke 4:1), Jesus repeats the story of Israel. Upon entering the Promised Land, God charged the nation of Israel to eradicate their enemies, the Canaanites, yet they failed to expunge them from the land (e.g., Judges 2:14). Jesus, though, faithfully resists the temptations during his forty-day testing and succeeds where Adam and Eve failed. His victory during his wilderness temptation is the initial defeat of the devil. Once Jesus is baptized, he enters the Promised Land, beginning his mission of establishing the new creation. Repeating the story of Adam and Eve and Israel, Jesus drives out Israel's true enemy, Satan, from the world and inaugurates the new creation.

According to Luke, the devil first attempts to break Jesus' trust in God's provision: "If you are the Son of God, tell this stone to become bread" (Luke 4:3). Remember that the book of Daniel predicts that Israel will undergo severe testing in the latter days and that a formidable enemy, an anti-prophet, will emerge on the scene who will deceive many within the nation (Daniel 11:31-35). It's beyond coincidence that Satan is here attempting to deceive Jesus in this end-time testing.

Satan wants Jesus to relinquish his trust in the Father and act independently of him. Jesus responds by quoting Deuteronomy 8:3: "Man shall not live on bread alone" (Luke 4:4). The Old Testament context of this verse is illuminating:

> [Israel,] Remember how the LORD your God led you all the way in the wilderness these forty years, to humble and test you in order to know what was in your heart, whether or not you would keep his commands. He humbled you, causing you to hunger and then feeding you with manna, which neither you nor your ancestors had known, to teach you that *man does not live on bread alone but on every word that comes from the mouth of the LORD.* (Deuteronomy 8:2-3)

The point of the quotation from Deuteronomy 8 is to demonstrate that Israel was to trust solely in God for all provision and care, both spiritual and physical. When Israel took things into her own hands, she failed miserably (e.g., Numbers 11).

As prophets, Adam and Eve were also responsible to hold fast to God's law (Genesis 1:28; 2:16-17) and relate it to every aspect of life. But as soon as the serpent approached Eve in the garden, she failed to believe the veracity of God's word and apply it to her encounter. The serpent undermined God's law by misquoting it (Genesis 3:1), and Eve failed to catch him in his treachery. Notice how Jesus is quick to quote Scripture in each encounter with Satan in the wilderness (Luke 4:4, 8, 12). He resists temptation by recounting and believing in God's Word. At no point in the temptation does Jesus tweak Scripture for his own selfish benefit. Without exception, the Word of God sustains and delivers.

This is one important reason why Christians must often meditate on the Bible. We must know God's promises to trust in them. Faith in the Word of God is critical. The apostle Paul argues that believers must "take up the shield of faith, with which you can extinguish all the flaming arrows of the evil one" (Ephesians 6:16). Belief in God's provision in Christ is a battle that we must wage daily, for if we do not, then our hearts will become cold and brittle.

The devil then takes Jesus to a place where they could see "in an instant all the kingdoms of the world," perhaps indicating that Jesus experienced this temptation in the form of a vision (Luke 4:5-8; cf. Revelation 4:1; 17:3; 21:10). The devil claims to have authority over the kingdoms of the earth and vows to give the earthly kingdoms over to Jesus if he worships him. The devil's exhortation to Jesus refers to a perpetual state of submission to and a ruling alongside of Satan. The type of worship that Satan desires is identical to the worship that God deserves and requires. Jesus responds to the devil's request by saying "Worship the Lord your God and serve him only" (Luke 4:8). This is a second quotation from Deuteronomy: "*Fear the* LORD *your God, serve him only* and take your oaths in his name" (Deuteronomy 6:13). Deuteronomy 6:13 requires Israel to maintain allegiance to God and to no one else, despite pressure from the surrounding nations. Unfortunately, Israel repeatedly succumbed to idolatry by worshiping other gods alongside of the Lord. This resulted in the Lord's punishing and eventual exiling Israel to Babylon.

Satan tempted Adam and Eve to become "like God, knowing good and evil" (Genesis 3:5). He tempts the first couple to betray God's image and become independent of God and function at his level. The temptation, at the heart of it, is to become like God—to rule and to think like God. Jesus recapitulates the same testing but, despite the enticements of the devil, remains faithful to God.

Each of us, no matter our circumstances, is tempted to worship everything but God. We are tempted to worship ourselves, our possessions, our children, our professions. Everything. I find in my own life that I'm especially drawn to worship my hobbies and interests. For example, I grew up playing sports nearly every day, so it's natural for me to get caught up in watching them or playing them as an adult. I live in Mississippi, the heart of SEC football. So I find myself thinking and talking about college football more than I do about the person of Christ. As enjoyable as it is to watch a game, I must come to grips that "eternal pleasures" (Psalm 16:11) are only found in the person of Christ.

For the last temptation, the devil takes Jesus to the "highest point of the temple," again, probably while Jesus experiences a vision (Luke 4:9-12). The devil tempts Jesus to cast himself from the temple's ledge, so that God will send his angels to protect him. The devil supplements his attack by quoting from Psalm 91:11-12:

> He will command his angels concerning you
>   to guard you carefully;
> they will lift you up in their hands,
>   so that you will not strike your foot against a stone. (Luke 4:10-11)

The devil desires to control God's provision by forcing his hand to protect the Son. In other words, Satan tempts Jesus to *manipulate* God. Jesus responds by saying, "Do not put the Lord your God to the test." He quotes one more text from Deuteronomy: "Do not follow other gods, the gods of the peoples around you; for the LORD your God, who is among you, is a jealous God and his anger will burn against you, and he will destroy you from the face of the land. *Do not put the LORD your God to the test* as you did at Massah" (Deuteronomy 6:14-16). The quotation from Deuteronomy 6:16 refers back to Exodus 17:1-7, where Israel demanded water from God instead of trusting in his provision. In the same way, Satan wants Jesus to demand that God save him from the fall from the temple.

At the heart of the third temptation is the temptation to act independently of God by forcing his hand. Instead of living in dependence of God in his image, Adam and Eve were tempted to assert authority outside of God's will. Recall that Adam and Eve were to rule on behalf of God over the created order; they were not to rule independently from God in any area of life. The serpent's promise that the first couple "be like God, knowing good and evil" likely refers to executing judgment outside of God. In their eyes, they desired to determine what is right and wrong. In the same way, Jesus is tested to live independently of his Father by manipulation. If Jesus flings himself over the temple, then he forces his Father to protect him. Unlike Adam and Israel, however, Jesus remains faithful by trusting in the Father's provision.

Ironically, Psalm 91:13, which immediately follows the passage quoted by Satan, says,

> You will tread on the lion and the cobra;
>   you will trample the great lion and the serpent.

Psalm 91 thus unpacks Genesis 3:15:

> And I will put enmity
>   between you and the woman,
>   and between your offspring and hers;
> *he will crush your head,*
>   *and you will strike his heel.*

Jesus, in his temptation, initially and decisively vanquishes Satan and "crushes his head," thus fulfilling Genesis 1:28 and 3:15, as well as Psalm 91:13!

Jesus' victory had ripple effects throughout the cosmos. Jesus slayed the devil not with military might but by faith in God's promises. Trust is mightier than the sword. The devil's defeat in the wilderness signaled the beginning of the destruction of his kingdom. Since the fall, Satan had enslaved the world under his rule. But now through the obedience of the last Adam and true Israel, Satan's rule is beginning to be displaced. Brandon Crowe nicely summarizes the significance of Jesus' temptation as follows:

> By setting Jesus's obedience in contrast to the failures of both Adam and Israel, the Evangelists communicate that Jesus's obedience surpasses the failures of his covenantal predecessors. The victory of Jesus over Satan in the wilderness realizes the obedience required of Israel. But this is not the end of the matter because, more fundamentally, Jesus's obedience in the wilderness fulfils the filial fealty required of Adam.[1]

---

[1] Brandon D. Crowe, *The Last Adam: A Theology of the Obedient Life of Jesus in the Gospels* (Grand Rapids: Baker Academic, 2017), 78.

Together with the cross and resurrection, Jesus' obedience during the wilderness temptation is the initial defeat of the devil.

MIGHTY IN WORD

In addition to his obedience in the wilderness temptation, Jesus also manifested his prophetic office by speaking and displaying God's truth to Israel. Adam and Israel's failure to announce the unvarnished truth anticipates Christ's faithful proclamation.

On the plains of Moab, Moses predicts that in the distant future God will "raise up for you a prophet like me. . . . You must listen to him" (Deuteronomy 18:15). Moses' prophecy is a response to Israel's plea in Deuteronomy 5:23-27, where the Israelites ask the Lord for a mediator who will stand in his glorious presence and faithfully communicate God's law to them. At Sinai, the nation of Israel was ghastly afraid of God's presence, so they plead for a mediator (Exodus 20:19).

In the transfiguration story, Mark alludes to Deuteronomy 18:15 when he records God's thunderous voice piercing through the cloud: "A voice came from the cloud: 'This is my Son, whom I love. *Listen to him!*'" (Mark 9:7). The transfiguration recalls Israel's experience at Sinai when God graciously gave them his law. By commanding the disciples to "listen" to Jesus, God is setting forth Jesus as the end-time prophet who will faithfully proclaim God's law. The teachings of Jesus are difficult to swallow at times, as his kingdom is not marked by political triumph but suffering and death. The disciples must trust in Jesus' kingdom message, even if it challenges the culture's most treasured traditions and expectations.

But Jesus is not simply a prophet. His teachings are on par with the Old Testament itself. He speaks as God himself spoke to the prophets of old. According to Mark 1:22, the crowds react in astonishment to Jesus' instruction: "The people were amazed at his teaching, because he taught them as one who had authority, not as the teachers of the law." Unlike the scholars of the day who merely interpreted Israel's Scriptures, Jesus is the very voice of God. Old Testament prophets spoke on behalf of God (e.g., Jeremiah 11:1-13); Jesus of Nazareth speaks as God. The same could be said for Jesus' seemingly bizarre prophetic behavior. When he curses the fig tree or heals a blind man with spittle, he does so as the Son of God. All of his behavior, his words and deeds, are wholly truthful and without error.

PASSING ON THE DIVINE IMAGE

The final dimension to Christ's prophetic image is taken from 1 Corinthians 15:42-53, one of the most insightful passages in all of the New Testament on the nature of Christ's glorified existence and his role in passing on his restored image to believers. It's hard to overstate the significance of this passage. What we discover here in 1 Corinthians 15 has been lurking in the background the last few chapters.

This section also bridges our discussion of Christ as the perfected Adam/ Israel (chaps. 5–7) and the church as the restored people of God in the following section (chaps. 8–10). We will first explore Christ as the last Adam in his resurrected body and then believers as little "last Adams" in their resurrected bodies.

Christ in his glorified Adamic body. Paul's lengthy discussion of the resurrection is due to some at Corinth who, probably because of their pagan worldview, doubted the doctrine of the resurrection (1 Corinthians 15:12). After defending the historical legitimacy of Christ's resurrection (1 Corinthians 15:1-11) and its relationship to the resurrection of believers (1 Corinthians 15:12-34), Paul moves on to the climax of the argument—the nature of the resurrection itself (1 Corinthians 15:35-57). It's here where we learn a great deal about Christ's glorified state in his resurrection body and about the resurrection bodies of all believers. Pertinent to my study, this passage tells us plainly about the perfected image of Christ and believers. In sum, it describes what it means to be part of restored humanity in the new creation.

In 1 Corinthians 15:42-45 Paul argues for a distinction between the earthly, corruptible body and the eternal, resurrected body of believers. One body is fit for the old age, and one body is fit for the new creation. Paul appeals to Genesis 2:7 to support this line of thinking: "If there is a natural body, there is also a spiritual body. So it is written: '*The first man Adam became a living being*'; *the last Adam, a life-giving Spirit.* The spiritual did not come first, but the natural, and after that the spiritual" (1 Corinthians 15:44-46). The terms *first* and *last* set a chronological distinction (old age and new age), whereas *natural* and *spiritual* reveal a spatial distinction (heaven and earth). Paul's interpretation of Genesis 2:7 fuses the temporal and spatial.

Remarkably, the prefall Adam of Genesis 2:7, from Paul's perspective, is still considered a "natural" or earthly being, though he had not yet sinned. The quotation from Genesis 2:7 is strategic. The fall of Adam and Eve doesn't occur until Genesis 3, so Paul argues that Adam, even *before* he sinned, was "earthly" and unfit for the new creation. This is to say that Adam, despite being sinless and perfectly created, was incomplete. For Adam and Eve to inhabit the new creation that housed the glory of God, they and the earth needed to be transformed into a glorified state. Such is the nature of God's glorious presence. It demands that all of creation be brought to a completely glorified existence.

This observation fits very well with the first two chapters in this book. There I argued that Adam and Eve were created in the divine image and that they were charged with extending God's presence beyond Eden by subduing the created order and establishing a godly line (Genesis 1:28; 2:15). They were also commanded what *not* to do—eat from the tree of the knowledge of good and evil (Genesis 2:17). Had the first couple been successful, God would have transformed creation and humanity into a glorified state so that they could dwell intimately with him for all of eternity.

Christ, however, has a different body from Adam and Eve. Before the resurrection, Christ identified with the earthly body of the prefall Adam. At the resurrection, the Spirit transforms Christ's body into a glorified existence. Christ's resurrected body is different from his earthly body. This may explain why the Gospels depict Jesus' disciples and followers having a difficult time recognizing their resurrected Lord (Luke 24:15-16; John 20:14; 21:4). This is not to say that Jesus' resurrected body was altogether radically different; some physical characteristics of Jesus appeared to have carried over to his glorified state (Luke 24:31). In his resurrected body, Jesus also enigmatically appears and vanishes before his disciples (Luke 24:31, 36; John 20:19, 26).

Christ was the first to transform into a glorified state, an existence that is fit to inhabit the heavens and the earth. He is, quite simply, the beginning of the new creation. As the perfected image of God, Christ's resurrected body is the same body that Adam and Eve would have inherited had they been faithful to God's law. This is precisely why Paul refers to Christ as the "last

Adam." The last Adam is greater than the first Adam in that he successfully accomplished the requirements God bestowed on the first couple.

It could be said that Jesus' body is a microcosm of the new heavens and earth. Revelation 3:14 labels Christ as the "Amen, the faithful and true Witness, the *Beginning* of the creation of God" (NASB). Consider the concrete applications of this truth to our daily lives. If Christ's resurrection is truly the beginning of the new cosmos, then God will certainly bring it to pass! God has never failed to finish what he starts. The world around us suffers decay and hostility, yet God has already begun the process of renewal through his Son.

Believers in their glorified Adamic bodies. We are now in a position to consider one of the most perplexing phrases in all of the New Testament—the last Adam is the "life-giving Spirit." Right away, we realize that this phrase doesn't match the phrase that precedes it: "So it is written: 'The first man Adam became a living being'; the last Adam, a life-giving spirit" (1 Corinthians 15:45). We expect the phrase "living Spirit," paralleling the first Adam's becoming a "living being." Something appears to be amiss. Why would Paul do such a thing? Not a few prominent commentators have expressed their consternation over this difficult change.

To answer this dilemma we must return to Genesis 1–5. In Genesis 2:7, God "breathed into his [Adam's] nostrils the breath of life, and the man became a living being." God's creative act here in Genesis 2 parallels his creative act in Genesis 1:26-28, where he creates Adam and Eve in his image. So, as the narrative intimates, receiving the "breath of life" (or "spirit of life") is nearly synonymous with being created in God's image.

The key to unlocking the difficult phrase "life-giving Spirit" in 1 Corinthians 15:45 lies in a careful reading of Genesis 5:1-3. In chapter two I observed the tight connection between Genesis 1:26-28 and Genesis 5:1-2 (see table 7.1).

GEN 1:26-28 NASB	GEN 5:1-2 NASB
Then God said, "Let Us make man in Our image, according to *Our likeness*"; . . . *God created man* in his own image, in the image of God *he created him; male and female he created them. God blessed them.*	This is the book of the generations of Adam. In the day when *God created man*, He made him in the *likeness of God*. He *created them male and female*, and *he blessed them* and named them Man in the day when *they were created*.

Table 7.1

Just as God imparted his image to Adam, so also Adam imparts his image to Seth. Genesis 5 is intended to be read in light of Genesis 1:26-28, as a continuation or fulfillment, implying that Adam's descendants have begun to "rule" and "subdue" the earth. By passing on his image to Seth, Adam is obeying God's command in Genesis 1:28: "Be fruitful and increase in number; fill the earth and subdue it." Adam and Eve are beginning to fulfill their threefold office. If Adam's receiving the breath of life parallels his being created in God's image, then perhaps it's not a leap to suggest that Adam passes along this breath of life, or image, to Seth. We now have most of the ingredients for understanding Paul's labeling Christ as the "life-giving Spirit."

Putting all the pieces together, just as the first Adam imparts his image to Seth and continues the line of blessing, so now the last Adam imparts his image to believers, giving them eschatological and consummate blessing. Christ is the greater Adam, passing along his image to his sons in the same way the first Adam passed along his image to Seth. A close reading of 1 Corinthians 15:49, just a few verses after the Genesis 2:7 quotation in 1 Corinthians 15:45 yields the Old Testament allusion seen in table 7.2.

GENESIS 5:3	1 CORINTHIANS 15:49
When Adam had lived 130 years, he had a son in his own likeness, in his own *image*; and he named him Seth. (emphasis added)	And just as we have borne the *image* of the earthly man, so shall we bear the *image* of the heavenly man. (emphasis added)

Table 7.2

Paul contends that believers will, at the resurrection, bear the image of the last Adam or represent him in their appearance.[2] "Bearing" or "donning" the image of the last Adam parallels Seth's receiving Adam's image.

So why does Paul label Christ as the "life-giving Spirit"? Just like Adam's passing along his image to Seth, at the second coming, Christ will pass along his image to believers and clothe them with bodies that are fit for the new creation. We will have the same perfected image of Christ, the last Adam! Perhaps the reason Paul argues that Jesus is a life-giving *Spirit* stems from the dominant role of the Holy Spirit in the process of creation.

---

[2]Walter Bauer, "φορέω," *BDAG* 1064.

Just as the Spirit was active in the first creation (Genesis 1:2), so will he be in the new creation.

CONCLUSION AND APPLICATION

Christ demonstrated his role as a prophet in his faithful embodiment of God's law during his forty-day wilderness temptation. At every point, Jesus was faithful where Adam and Israel were not. His relentless faith in God's promises vanquished the devil and broke his grip on the world. Jesus' prophetic role was also evident in his being God's mouthpiece to the world. But we learned that Jesus functioned not only as a traditional prophet but also as God himself. Jesus' words are God's words. My last point pertained to Christ as the last Adam who was transformed into his glorified body at the resurrection. He is the beginning of the new cosmos.

I will now attempt to synthesize all that we have covered in the first seven chapters: (1) Christ is the perfected, last Adam. Because of his obedience in his life, death, and resurrection, he received a glorified body. This is the same body that Adam and Eve were promised had they perfectly obeyed. (2) At the very end of history, when Christ returns, he will pass along his perfected image to believers, transforming them fully into the same glorified existence that he enjoys. There will certainly be some differences, since Christ is divine and we are not. We will not possess attributes endemic to God alone (omniscience, sovereign power, etc.). We will be finally and fully kings, priests, and prophets, but we will not be *divine* kings, priests, and prophets. The distinction between Creator and creature will remain. We will serve on behalf of God and continue to operate as God's images in the new creation. (3) Paul is not advocating a return to Eden, as many presume. Paul looks beyond Eden. He looks toward the cosmic Eden, where the entire universe is one gigantic temple-city filled with God's glory. (4) All of humanity is in the image of either the first Adam or the last Adam. There is no in-between. Fundamentally, what it means to be part of the true people of God, true humanity, and true Israel is to inherit the perfected image of the last Adam. The restored image of God is the distinguishing mark of being a son or daughter of God, trumping all forms of ethnicity.

RECOMMENDED READING

Crowe, Brandon D. *The Last Adam: A Theology of the Obedient Life of Jesus in the Gospels*. Grand Rapids: Baker Academic, 2017.

Witherington, Ben, III. *Jesus the Sage: The Pilgrimage of Wisdom*. Minneapolis: Fortress, 2000.

Wright, N. T. *Jesus and the Victory of God*. Christian Origins and the Question of God 2. Minneapolis: Fortress, 1996.

Chapter Eight

THE CHURCH AS KINGS

THE PREVIOUS THREE CHAPTERS highlighted Christ as the perfected image of God—the true king, priest, and prophet. His mission succeeded where Adam and Israel failed. God's commission to Adam and Israel was successfully achieved through Christ's obedience throughout his life, especially in his crucifixion and resurrection. This is why the Gospel writers exert so much energy connecting Jesus' career to the nation of Israel in the Old Testament. He must undo their wrongs. But Jesus' obedient life extends to his followers. God applies Christ's obedience to the covenant made with Adam and Israel to the church. The church is, through union with Christ, little last Adams and true Israelites. We reap the benefits of his work. We are what he is. Since he is the perfected image of God, the church is the corporate perfected image of God.

The present chapter and the next two explore our identity as kings, priests, and prophets. These three chapters lean heavily on our union with Christ and the conviction that the "latter days" have truly broken into history. If we are indeed united to Christ and his work, then we should not be surprised that his identity is appropriated to all of his followers. We are, after all, little Christs or "Christians." The church's corporate nature of being the perfected image of God is a robustly eschatological event. The Old Testament anticipated that this day would arrive, and it has initially taken place in Christ. The goal of this chapter is to explain, albeit briefly, how the New Testament views our identity as end-time kings ruling in God's kingdom.

THE KINGSHIP OF BELIEVERS IN THE GOSPELS AND ACTS

In chapter five, on Jesus as the long-awaited King of Israel, I mentioned how the New Testament is quick to point out the scope and manner of his rule. Exceeding Jewish expectations, he rules not primarily only over a parcel of land in the Middle East but over the entire cosmos. The way in which he rules also differs from expectations. His rule is paradoxically not marked by political strength but by suffering and death. On the cross, at the moment of defeat and shame, Jesus is exalted and reigns supreme over the far reaches of the universe.

The Gospels also underscore the kingly rule of Jesus' followers. Jesus' life, death, and resurrection spearhead God's rule and reign on the earth, and all those who trust in him participate in his rule. The cosmic rule of Christ flows and extends through his followers on the earth. The original commission of Genesis 1:28 is fulfilled first in Christ and then in the church. Jesus began to subdue Satan and his demons, and his disciples follow suit.

Appointing the Twelve. All three Synoptic Gospels present the appointing of the twelve disciples, and two of the Gospels, Mark and Luke, specify that the appointing took place on a mountain (Mark 3:13; Luke 6:12). Often in the Old Testament, God's presence is associated with mountains. The Garden of Eden, as we saw in chapter one, was the first mountain where God dwelled and manifested his glorious presence to Adam and Eve (Genesis 2:8-14; Ezekiel 28:13-14). Sinai is also portrayed as a grand temple on which God resides (Exodus 3:5; 19–24). Mountains also feature prominently in the latter days, as Isaiah prophesies that Israel and the nations will stream to the "mountain of the LORD's temple" in the "last days" (Isaiah 2:2; cf. Micah 4:7).

As God fashioned and commissioned Adam in the garden and the nation of Israel at Sinai, so too Jesus fashions and commissions true Israel on a mountain. But the failure of Adam and Israel paves the way for the success of Christ and his followers. With Satan initially defeated, the long-awaited Messiah appoints twelve disciples to reconstitute the twelve tribes of Israel and expel demons from the land. Jesus "appointed twelve that they might be with him and that he might send them out to preach and to have authority to drive out demons" (Mark 3:14-15). The Twelve grab onto the coattails of Jesus, their king, and are empowered to conquer the enemy. His victory is their victory.

The disciples must assume their identity as kings and rulers in God's kingdom by welcoming the nations into the community of faith. The disciples will not fight with swords and spears but with the good news of the cross and resurrection. Genuine subjugation of evil can only be achieved through the message of Christ's saving work.

Acts 1:8. The Great Commission in Matthew 28 is not a far cry from Acts 1:8. This verse, perhaps one of the most well-known passages in the New Testament, is brimming with insight related to the restoration of God's image in humanity: "But you will receive power when the Holy Spirit comes on you; and you will be my witnesses in Jerusalem, and in all Judea and Samaria, and to the ends of the earth." Acts 1:8 is tied to the disciples' question about the restoration of the kingdom (Acts 1:6). They wonder if the theocratic nation of Israel will be restored right then and there. The disciples consider whether Jesus is going to establish his physical kingdom by judging the pagan Romans and releasing Israel from physical and spiritual bondage. But Jesus' reply is nothing short of astounding: "It is not for you to know the times or dates the Father has set by his own authority" (Acts 1:7).

Even though the disciples do not have the prerogative to know *when* the kingdom will be set up, Jesus indeed answers their question, albeit indirectly, in Acts 1:8. Jesus responds to their question about when the kingdom will be set up by asserting that the pouring out of the Spirit will demonstrate the presence of the end-time kingdom. The gift of the Spirit, according to the Old Testament, is one of the hallmarks of the in-breaking of the kingdom of God. The Spirit is also tied to God's power in the original creation (Genesis 1:2) and in the new creation (Isaiah 34:14-15).

The prophet Ezekiel portrays the restoration of Israel through the use of resurrection language. It is striking that his description most likely alludes to Genesis 2 and the creation of Adam and Eve: "This is what the Sovereign LORD says: My people, I am going to open your graves and bring you up from them. . . . Then you, my people, will know that I am the Lord, when I open your graves and bring you up from them. *I will put my Spirit in you and you will live, and I will settle you in your own land*" (Ezekiel 37:12-14; see Ezekiel 37:1-11). These texts and others like them associate the Spirit with God's great act of creating. Just as the Spirit played a vital role in the original creation, so too he will play a role in the end-time new creation.

So the promise of the Spirit descending on the disciples in Acts 1:8 means that God is creating anew and ushering in the final stage of redemption. Jesus' life, death, and resurrection inaugurated the new age, but here in Acts 1–2 this new age gains considerable momentum through the Spirit's work in and through the apostles. Though the apostles had already received an initial dose of the Spirit soon after the resurrection and had their divine images initially restored (John 20:19-23), Pentecost signals a formal progression in how they will operate as the true people of God in the new age.

But how will the apostles concretely function as the restored people of God? The Twelve are primarily to be his witnesses by taking the gospel to the ends of the earth. Acts 1:8 is a fitting summary of the book of Acts—through the proclamation of the gospel, God's glory will be taken to the far corners of the known world in fulfillment of Genesis 1:28. Adam and Eve's primary goal in bearing God's image as kings, priests, and prophets was to extend God's glory to every inch of the earth. All three offices work toward this ultimate goal. The pouring out of the Spirit here in Acts 2 ensures that Christ will be proclaimed to Israel and the nations, resulting in the restoration of humanity.

Just as God breathed into Adam the "breath of life" and gave his presence to Israel at Sinai, God poured out his Spirit on Christ at the Jordan River. Then, at Pentecost, God pours out his Spirit once more on humanity, restoring his image within them. James Dunn reasons, "What Jordan was to Jesus, Pentecost was to the disciples. As Jesus entered the new age and covenant by being baptized in the Spirit at Jordan, so the disciples followed him in like manner at Pentecost."[1]

---

[1]James D. G. Dunn, *Baptism in the Holy Spirit: A Re-examination of the New Testament Teaching on the Gift of the Spirit in Relation to Pentecostalism Today* (Philadelphia: Westminster, 1970), 40.

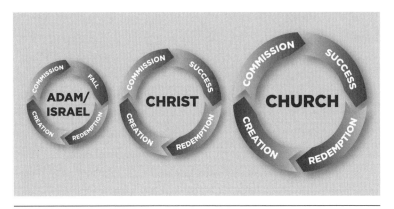

Figure 8.1

Pentecost is the formal event in which God restores humanity to function as kings, priests, and prophets. The perfected image of Christ is formally passed on to the disciples (Acts 2:1-4), then to Israel (Acts 2:5-41; 8:14-17; 19:1-6), and then to the nations (Acts 10:1–11:18).

As kings, the apostles and the church herald the good news of Christ's death and resurrection to unbelievers. Only the gospel can deliver sinners from their plight and overcome the power of evil. The book of Acts narrates how the apostles battle the enemies of God. They will do so not with political might but with the message of the cross. As difficult as it was for the Jewish people to be under the political thumb of Rome, that paled in comparison to their true state of affairs—being enslaved to sin and the devil. The Jews longed for the coming Messiah, would who deliver them from Rome's oppression, but what they failed to realize was the extent of sin's oppression in their own lives. As the book of Acts unfolds, we learn how the gospel conquers, defeats, and subdues sin in the lives of all humanity.

Pentecost and the restoration of the divine image in humanity. Pentecost, one of the most significant events in the history of redemption, relates to how the church is fashioned in the restored image of God. Pentecost is so significant that we will examine it from three different vantage points: the church as the end-time kings (chap. 8), priests (chap. 9), and prophets (chap. 10). In chapter two we learned that the fall doesn't erase God's image in humanity, but it does pervert it. Each person, believer and unbeliever, still retains the threefold offices of king, priest, and prophet. A key difference between the two, though, is that the believer's image is beginning to be restored so that it starts to function as it was originally intended—representing God in all facets of life.

Every Old Testament believer operated as a king, priest, and prophet at some level within the Israelite community. For example, each righteous Israelite executed their office as king when they ruled over sin in their personal lives, as priest when they removed all instances of defilement from their home, and as prophet when they embodied God's law and shared it with their families and others. But under the old covenant, these three offices were officially split into three to serve the nation of Israel (Deuteronomy 17–18). The Spirit empowered prophets, priests, and kings to perform their specific duties for the nation. We can conclude, then, that each Old Testament saint executed their threefold office on a personal level but not on a political or national level.

The Gospels and Acts narrate a considerable transition: the movement from a theocracy to a community. Like playing a Jenga game, Jesus removed key foundational pieces of Israel's theocracy, leading to its eventual collapse. The political, theocratic nation of Israel came under judgment for their continued refusal to obey God. This happened on two levels: (1) spiritually, God's judgment was poured out on the nation throughout Jesus' ministry, climaxing at the crucifixion (1 Thessalonians 2:16); (2) physically, the Romans conquered the nation just a few decades later in AD 70. The theocratic dimension of Israel came to an end in the first century and will never be reestablished.[2] Pentecost captures both of these dimensions at some level: judgment on the nation of Israel and the restoration of the true people of God.

The pouring out of the Spirit in fulfillment of Old Testament prophecies (e.g., Joel 2) signals the restoration of the threefold office for all of God's people. This renewal began with Jesus' own personal Pentecost at his baptism and then progressed to his followers (see fig. 8.2).

[2]For a discussion of this difficult issue, see Hans K. LaRondelle, *The Israel of God in Prophecy: Principles of Prophetic Interpretation* (Berrien Springs, MI: Andrews University Press, 1983), 124-34.

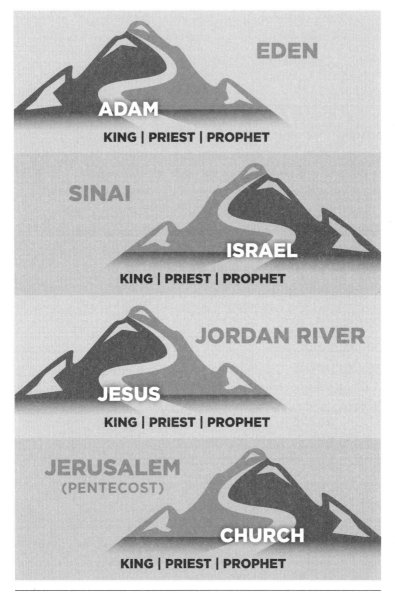

Figure 8.2

Though every Old Testament saint enjoyed the threefold office of king, priest, and prophet on a personal level, the New Testament believer does so in a greater way. The threefold office of each New Testament believer seems to operate in a greater capacity than it did with Old Testament believers in primarily two ways: (1) Every New Testament believer enjoys a restored image of God, an image that goes beyond Adam's original image (1 Corinthians 15:45-49). Therefore, believers in the new age can execute their threefold office through Christ, in a more effective manner on the personal level. That is, the restored image in New Testament believers is eschatological to the core. We rule over all forms of evil in our daily lives, enjoy God's presence, and embody God's law far more than Adam and the nation of Israel ever did. (2) Our restored image takes on a more prominent role in the world. Each New Testament believer is, through Christ, in solidarity with every other believer. So the church functions as a united, corporate Adam that rules over the onslaught of hostility from the unbelieving world. Believers do so not with physical might but, ironically and paradoxically, through suffering. We overcome the world spiritually by being overcome physically. The church also functions both as a corporate priest to the world by sharing the gospel and mediating God's glory to the nations and as a corporate prophet by faithfully obeying God's Word and embodying it to their neighbors.

THE KINGSHIP OF BELIEVERS IN PAUL

Romans 16. At the end of Romans, Paul warns the church to avoid those who create division within the community of faith (Romans 16:17-18). Believers at Rome must be "wise about what is *good*, and innocent about what is *evil*" (Romans 16:19). The wording here calls to mind Genesis 2:17: "You must not eat from the tree of the knowledge of *good and evil*, for when you eat from it you will certainly die" (cf. Genesis 3:5).[3] The result of partaking of the forbidden fruit in the garden was knowledge apart from God. But here in Romans 16:19 Paul ironically uses Genesis 2:17 as a reference to true wisdom that is subordinate to God's law—God's way of thinking. The fall produced a perverted wisdom that stands apart from God, but Christ's redemption paves the way for genuinely understanding the world around us. It's thinking God's thoughts after him. Paul tells the Romans that they are a better version

---

[3]Mark. A. Seifrid, argues for an allusion to Genesis 3:5 but not to Genesis 2:17, though these two passages are inextricably linked ("Romans," in *Commentary on the New Testament Use of the Old Testament*, ed. G. K. Beale and D. A. Carson [Grand Rapids: Baker Academic, 2007], 692).

of Adam and Eve and that they can indeed hold fast to God's wisdom in service to the church. In the immediate context, such wisdom pertains to weeding out false teaching in the local community of believers (Romans 16:17).

Genesis 3 remains uppermost in Paul's mind, as the following verse promises that God "will soon crush Satan under your feet" (Romans 16:20). The language harks back to the promise of Genesis 3:15:

> I will put enmity
> between you and the woman,
> and between your offspring and hers;
> *he will crush your head,*
> and you will strike his heel.

God promised Adam and Eve that a godly king, who is in the pristine image of God, will vanquish the serpent at the very end of history. This king will accomplish what Adam and Eve failed to accomplish. They failed to rule over the serpent and rid Eden of it, so a faithful descendant arose and obeyed where they disobeyed. At the beginning of Romans, Paul identifies Christ as the long-awaited "descendant of David" who was "appointed the Son of God in power by his resurrection from the dead" (Romans 1:3-4). At the heart of the gospel, then, is Christ's victory over Satan. This victory was anticipated "in the Holy Scriptures," a reference, at least in part, to Genesis 3:15 (Romans 1:2). Thus at the beginning of Romans Paul underscores Jesus' victory over sin and the devil, and at the end of Romans he highlights the church's victory over wickedness and the powers of evil. The victory Jesus initially achieved at the cross and resurrection fulfilled the great promise of Genesis 3:15 and continues to be fulfilled in the church.

Genuine Christians should be characterized by the defeat of sin in their lives. Paul puts his finger on the matter when he asks, "We are those who have died to sin; how can we live in it any longer?" (Romans 6:2). If we are truly kings, then our lives will be patterned by righteousness and not wickedness. Christ delivered us to reign with him, not to be imprisoned in sin.

Ephesians 6. Paul concludes the book of Ephesians with a discussion of Christian armor that protects believers against the onslaught of Satan and his minions. Satan attempts to divide and breach the unity that believers enjoy with one another, so believers must "put on the full armor of God" (Ephesians 6:11). The following section (Ephesians 6:14-15, 17) contains considerable points of contact with the Old Testament, chief among them the book of Isaiah. According to Isaiah 59:17, the Lord

> put on righteousness as his breastplate
> and the helmet of salvation on his head.

The Lord promises to wage war against his enemies, so that "people will fear the name of the Lord" (Isaiah 59:18-19). Similar language is also found earlier in Isaiah, where it is said that the Messiah will enjoy a "belt" of "righteousness" (Isaiah 11:5). This end-time king will lay waste to God's enemies and judge Israel with faithfulness (Isaiah 11:4). One last prominent text is Isaiah 52:7, where the feet of the Lord's prophets are "beautiful," because they "proclaim peace" and "bring good tidings." These prophets herald the news that God has conquered Israel's enemies and established his end-time kingdom (Isaiah 52:9-10).

By applying these texts from Isaiah to the church, Paul argues that believers participate in the end-time battle that began with the person of Christ. Jesus triumphed over the devil, and Christians fight in the wake of that decisive victory against Satan and his allies. "Just as God waged warfare in the past to vindicate his name, to rescue his people or judge his people, so now God wages warfare against the powers through the church."[4] The devil and his minions continue to resist, though the final outcome is inevitable at Christ's second coming. Believers wage end-time warfare, declaring "peace" to the world that victory has indeed been achieved.

Peace here does not necessarily entail political peace but spiritual peace. The church is the vehicle by which God proclaims reconciliation to a lost and dying world. Do our lives testify to the reconciliation that takes place in Christ? If we have been truly reconciled to God through Christ, then our relationships with one another will inevitably follow suit. If, though, our lives are characterized by strife and fracture, then we have little assurance that we have been reconciled to God.

---

[4]Timothy G. Gombis, *The Drama of Ephesians: Participating in the Triumph of God* (Downers Grove, IL: IVP Academic, 2010), 158.

Christians must be prepared to fend off "the devil's schemes" in the "day of evil" (Ephesians 6:11, 13). In this respect, they are to make "the most of every opportunity, because the days are evil" (Ephesians 5:16). The end-time deceptive schemes of Satan arrived in the first century, and believers remain on alert (see Ephesians 4:14). According to the Old Testament, false teaching blossoms in the latter days, and many within the covenant community fall prey to such teaching (e.g., Daniel 11:32). Equipped with the armor of God, saints are empowered to overcome such devilish practices.

THE KINGSHIP OF BELIEVERS IN REVELATION

Revelation 7. The depiction of the church as the 144,000 in Revelation 7 is probably one of the most graphic portrayals of believers as kings in the New Testament. The introductory formula in 7:1, "after this," tells us that John saw the vision of chapter 7 *after* he saw the vision of Revelation 6. Revelation 7 explains how the church can survive the seal judgments outlined in Revelation 6. How can they withstand such end-time wrath? Because they have been protected and sealed (cf. Ezekiel 9:4-6). Notice that the sealing in Revelation takes place before the godly angels unleash the evil forces upon the earth. Revelation 7:3 reads, "Do not harm the land or the sea or the trees *until* we put a seal on the foreheads of the servants of our God."

John then describes numerically who will be sealed in the following verses: the 144,000. The number 144,000, though it may seem odd at first blush, makes good sense in light of the symbolic nature of Revelation. The number 144 appears to be derived from $12 \times 12 = 144$. The number twelve reflects the twelve tribes of Israel (Revelation 7:5-8). Multiplying 12×12 thus refers to *true* Israel. Last, $12 \times 12 \times 1,000 = 144,000$. The number 1,000 in Revelation refers to something completed or full (e.g., Revelation 20:1-7). So the number 144,000 symbolically depicts the church as the true Israel.

According to Richard Bauckham, the numbering of 144,000 in Revelation 7:4-8 suggests that those numbered are an army.[5] The list in Revelation 7 closely resembles the census lists in the book of Numbers that organize

---

[5]Richard Bauckham, *The Climax of Prophecy: Studies in the Book of Revelation* (Edinburgh: T&T Clark, 1993), 217-29.

Israel into an army to conquer the Promised Land. For example, compare
the distribution between Numbers 1 and Revelation 7, as seen in table 8.1.

NUMBERS 1	REVELATION 7
1:21 "The number from the tribe of **Reuben** was 46,500."	7:5 "from the tribe of **Reuben** 12,000"
1:23 "The number from the tribe of **Simeon** was 59,300."	7:7 "from the tribe of **Simeon** 12,000"
1:25 "The number from the tribe of **Gad** was 45,650."	7:5 "from the tribe of **Gad** 12,000"
1:27 "The number from the tribe of **Judah** was 74,600."	7:5 "From the tribe of **Judah** 12,000 were sealed"
1:29 "The number from the tribe of **Issachar** was 54,400."	7:7 "from the tribe of **Issachar** 12,000"

Table 8.1

At the end of the list, Numbers 1:45 states, "All the Israelites twenty years
old or more *who were able to serve in Israel's army* were counted according
to their families." The census was taken so that the nation of Israel could
prepare for battle as they entered the Promised Land and waged war against
the idolatrous Canaanites.

The similarities between these two lists and others (e.g., Numbers 26:5-51)
are striking. By invoking the census list, John is depicting the church as a
powerful army ready to conquer their enemies and enter the true Promised
Land, that is, the new creation. The second half of the vision, Revelation 7:9-17,
interprets the first half. The first half depicts God's people as true Israel, and
the second half explains that the 144,000 are made up of "every nation, tribe,
people and language" (Revelation 7:9). The true Israel of God comprises all
the nations. All those who enjoy a restored image of God can be sure that
they are counted among the 144,000.

The second half of the vision portrays the 144,000 in their resurrected,
glorified state in the new heavens and earth and informs us *how* they got
there—they "washed their robes and made them white in the blood of the
Lamb" (Revelation 7:14). God's people ruled as kings over the world and all
of its pernicious entrapments by being physically persecuted by it. Believers
primarily rule through their faithfulness to Christ and the gospel.

CONCLUSION AND APPLICATION

We learned that the church comprises individuals who bear the restored image of God, the true Israel. We are corporate kings, priests, and prophets, tasked with ruling, mediating God's presence, and obeying God's law. But if the church is true Israel, then what of the nation of Israel? Will God restore the nation immediately preceding the second coming of Christ? These are difficult questions, and evangelicals differ on how to answer them. Dispensationalists are fundamentally convinced that God is not done with Israel. They argue that God will keep his promises to the patriarchs by restoring the nation and physically bringing them back into the Promised Land.

Engaging this complex debate is outside the scope of this project, but I will offer two brief comments. First, the people of God begins, not with Israel, but with Adam and Eve. God promises to preserve a people group, a community of those restored in his image, in Genesis 3, and we see the initial fulfillment of this with Seth in Genesis 5:1-3. The nation of Israel, therefore, is *part* of a covenant people of God at large, a community of individuals who possess the restored image of God. Second, the Old Testament, as far as I can tell, never talks about the restoration of the *theocratic nation* of Israel. Indeed, the pattern that the Bible sets forth is the restoration of only a remnant. From the beginning of the Old Testament and throughout the New Testament, the people of God never have been and never will be the majority (e.g., Isaiah 11:16; 37:32; Jeremiah 23:3; 31:7; Micah 5:7-8; Zephaniah 2:7-9; Romans 11:1-5). Moreover, God poured out his wrath with great finality on the nation of Israel when they crucified Christ (1 Thessalonians 2:16), so the theocratic nation of Israel has come to an end.

Under the Mosaic administration, God's people were defined by externals— physical structures (e.g., the physical temple), their diet, Sabbath observance, circumcision, and so on. But now that Christ has come all of Israel's theocratic institutions and laws find their ultimate fulfillment in him. So has the church *replaced* Israel? Though some theologians believe so, I'm not convinced. Much of Paul's argument in Romans 9–11 appears to take issue with the role of ethnic Jews. Christian Gentiles stand on equal footing with ethnic Jews, but that does not preclude the salvation of a remnant of ethnic Jews throughout history. True Israel is composed of a remnant of Christian Gentiles and a remnant of Christian Jews.

How can we apply this precious truth of our identity as end-time believers to our daily lives? I can think of at least two ways. The first is on a practical, "earthly," or physical level. Since believers now enjoy a restored image, we ought to exercise rule over the created order. What does this look like concretely? We continue to fulfill the creation mandate given to Adam in Genesis 1:28 by caring for this earth in a responsible way. According to the EPA, the average American in 2013 generated about 1,600 pounds of trash a year. That's staggering. We should be mindful of living in excess and consuming more than we need. And recycling waste, though it may seem insignificant in the broad scheme of things, is indicative of one's broader outlook on their relationship with the created order. Anthony Hoekema is therefore right to claim, "The renewal of the image means . . . that man is now enabled properly to rule over and care for God's creation. That is to say, he is now empowered to exercise dominion over the earth and over nature in a responsible, obedient, and unselfish way."[6] Yes, this earth will eventually be transformed into a new cosmos (2 Peter 3:10), but we, as those who image God in the created order, should be thoughtful of God's commitment to the creation and our role within it.

The second way in which we can apply our identity as kings is on a spiritual level. Adam and Eve were created for the purpose of extending God's rule over the created order, so that his divine presence would radiate out from them. Through Christ, we now rule over spiritual realities. Paul claims in Ephesians 6:12 that "our struggle is not against flesh and blood, but against the rulers, against the authorities, against the powers of this dark world and against the spiritual forces of evil in the heavenly realms." We are to rule over everything that is hostile to the Christian life. This principle is often tied to lies and deceit, well-used weapons of the devil. Christians must learn God's Word and learn it well, so that as we engage the world and encounter its trickery we may parry Satan's attack. In Christ we have already achieved victory, but we must continue to bring all of life into conformity with God's will.

---

[6]Anthony A. Hoekema, *Created in God's Image* (Grand Rapids: Eerdmans, 1986), 88.

RECOMMENDED READING

Beasley-Murray, G. R. *Jesus and the Kingdom of God*. Grand Rapids: Eerdmans, 1986.

Moo, Douglas J., and Jonathan A. Moo. *Creation Care: A Biblical Theology of the Natural Life*. Grand Rapids: Zondervan, 2018.

Poythress, Vern S. *Understanding Dispensationalists*. 2nd ed. Phillipsburg, NJ: P&R, 1993.

Chapter Nine

THE CHURCH AS PRIESTS

WE LEARNED IN the previous chapter that Pentecost signaled the creation of a new humanity, the beginning of the restored people of God. Just as God created Adam and Eve on the mountain of Eden and Israel on Mount Sinai, so he fashioned a new humanity in the image of Christ in Jerusalem. The Spirit descended on the church, empowering it to fulfill its identity as kings, priests, and prophets. One key difference remains between the church and Adam and Israel in the Old Testament: the church is the eschatological people of God. Though standing in continuity with Adam and the nation of Israel, the church enjoys a perfected or restored divine image, albeit in an inaugurated sense. While God certainly dwelt with Adam and Eve and with the Israelites in the temple, God dwells with new covenant believers in a far more intimate way. We've seen throughout this project a strong connection between God's glory and his people as images, designed to exist in his presence. To be human is to enjoy God's glory and honor him in all we say and do. It is this dimension that we will now explore briefly. My purpose here is to uncover the church's identity as priests who enjoy God's presence and are committed to mediating it to the nations.

THE PRIESTHOOD OF BELIEVERS
IN THE GOSPELS AND ACTS

A chief aspect of Jesus' ministry was to show that he functions as the new temple of God. The physical temple in Jerusalem, as attractive as it was in the ancient world, with its unrivaled beauty, was incapable of housing God's glory in its fullness and was powerless in providing complete atonement for sin. Recall, too, that the earthly temple was a symbol of a greater reality—the cosmic temple. Each tier of the temple corresponds to a cosmic reality: the outer courts symbolized the earth (Exodus 20:24-25; 1 Kings 7:23-25), the holy place signified the visible heavens (Genesis 1:14; Exodus 25:8-9), and the holy of holies represented the invisible heavens, where God dwells with his angels (Exodus 25:18-22; Isaiah 6:1-7). The structure of the temple presents a symbolic story of God's ultimate intention to dwell with his people and creation. By arranging the temple in a three-tiered structure, from the most holy to the least holy, God discloses his plan of redemption. The miniature cosmos looks up and forward. It looks up as it corresponds to the cosmos, and it looks forward as it corresponds to God's plan of redemption. The cosmic design of the temple indicates that this presence will eventually break out from the heavenly holy of holies and fill every nook and cranny of the new cosmos.

Living water. The four Gospels bring the theme of the temple to a climax in the person of Christ. He is deemed "Immanuel"—God with us (Matthew 1:23). Heaven has come down in Jesus of Nazareth, and God is now keeping his promise to dwell intimately with humanity and creation. But now that the glory of God has descended, the physical temple in Jerusalem is outmoded. There's no sense putting new wine in old wineskins. The Jerusalem temple even reeked of idolatry, so God judged the earthly temple with great finality (John 2:19). Why worship in a building where God is experienced only in part, when God's true presence is found in Christ? From the very beginning, God's intention has always been to dwell in and among his people—not in buildings.

Running throughout the narrative of the Gospels is the idea that Jesus and his followers constitute the true temple. The disciples of Jesus become part of the end-time sanctuary of God. At the Festival of Booths, Jesus enigmatically declares, "Whoever believes in me, as Scripture has said, rivers of living water will flow from within them" (John 7:38; cf. John 4:14).[1] Jesus here references a string of passages from several Old Testament prophets that anticipate God dwelling with his people in the new creation. Water and temple go hand in hand (Genesis 2:10; Revelation 22:1-2). Zechariah 14:8 states, "On that day *living water* will flow out from Jerusalem, half of it east to the Dead Sea and half of it west to the Mediterranean Sea." At the end of the oracle, Zechariah predicts that "every pot in Jerusalem and Judah will be holy" because the entire city will be one gigantic temple (Zechariah 14:21; cf. Ezekiel 47:1-12). Jesus sees himself as the holy of holies, the true temple of God, and all those who believe in him will likewise become part of that sacred space. The glory of God that is found in its fullness in Jesus will, through the Spirit, inhabit his followers.

Pentecost and the church as the true temple. Pentecost, as I argued in the previous chapter, should be seen as the beginning of a new epoch in the history of redemption. God creates the end-time people of God in his image and fills them with his Spirit, just like he did with Adam and Israel. A chief difference remains between the church and Adam and the nation of Israel in the Old Testament. The church is the restored people of God, the eschatological true Israel. Despite Adam and the nation of Israel being created in God's image, they did not enjoy the *eschatological* image of God. Through the success of Christ's earthly ministry, his work on the cross, and his resurrection as the last Adam, God begins the process of creating a new humanity. In the last chapter I highlighted the royal dimension of the church's being created in the image of God. Now we turn to the church's corporate, priestly role. The book of Acts, especially in its description of Pentecost, presents the church as priests of God worshiping in the end time.

The appearance of "tongues as of fire" tangibly attests to the descent of the Spirit (Acts 2:3 NASB). In the Old Testament fire is often associated with God's presence, and this is especially true in Israel's exodus from Egypt and at Sinai (e.g., Exodus 13:21-22; 14:24; 19:18). Moreover, the combination of tongues and fire evokes a handful of passages that attest to God descending

---

[1]An alternate translation renders John 7:38 in the following manner: "As Scripture has said, rivers of living water will flow from him." It's somewhat unclear if Jesus is the focus of John 7:38 ("him" or those who trust in him ["them"]).

in judgment (see Isaiah 5:24-25; 30:27-30; cf. Matthew 3:11). Taking these clues together, we learn that God's heavenly presence descends on the church. It is here at Pentecost where the church officially becomes the end-time temple of God.[2]

In chapter one we discovered that God created the cosmos so that he could dwell in it and fill it with his glory. The ultimate intention is for God to dwell intimately with his people and his creation in an environment free from sin and wickedness. Christ's death judged the old creation, and his resurrection spearheaded the new creation. It was necessary for Christ to renew the cosmos, so that God could finally achieve his original goal that he set forth in Genesis 1–2. With Christ ascended on the throne in heaven (Acts 1:9-11), the Spirit is sent to fill creation with God's presence and dwell with God's people. As strange as it might seem, God's awesome presence dwells more intimately with each New Testament believer than it ever did with Adam and Eve in the garden or the nation of Israel at Sinai.

Commentators are quick to point out the parallels between Pentecost and God's revealing himself to Israel at Sinai (e.g., Exodus 19:16-20; 20:18).[3] I briefly discussed in chapter three how Sinai should be considered a large sanctuary and the top of the mountain as the holy of holies. That observation works quite well here in Acts 2, where Luke presents Pentecost as a greater Sinai. Indeed, the Jewish Feast of Pentecost (or the Feast of Weeks) celebrated the giving of the law at Sinai in the first century. "Just as Moses climbed Mount Sinai and received God's law, which he passed on to Israel, accompanied by visible signs of God's presence, Jesus ascended to God's right hand and poured out the gift of God's Spirit on the people of the new covenant."[4]

As the narrative of Acts unfolds, the church begins to grasp the significance of their new status as the end-time temple of God. The divine image in humanity flourishes in the presence of God. Where he goes, they go. Acts 5 begins with a seemingly odd event concerning Ananias and Sapphira (Acts 5:1-11). The couple's deception and God's subsequent judgment on them

---

[2]G. K. Beale, *The Temple and the Church's Mission: A Biblical Theology of the Dwelling Place of God*, NSBT 17 (Downers Grove, IL: IVP Academic, 2004), 201-44.
[3]E.g., Richard I. Pervo, *Acts: A Commentary*, Hermeneia 65P (Minneapolis: Fortress, 2009), 61.
[4]Eckhard J. Schnabel, *Acts*, ZECNT (Grand Rapids: Zondervan, 2012), 123.

demonstrates that sin within the covenant community, the newly established temple of God, will not be tolerated. The Mosaic covenant dictated in detail how the priests should keep the temple free from defilement, so that God may dwell with Israel. Since we are all priests serving in God's temple and his glory is in our midst, sin must be avoided at all cost. Each believer must embrace their identity as being in God's image and execute their office as a priest. Our priestly status is an immense privilege yet a terrifying responsibility. Unclean and wicked behavior has no business in the holy sanctuary of the church.

One way in which we can apply our identity as end-time priests is in our homes and local churches. As priests we need to be on the lookout for all things unclean in our places of worship and living. Do our habits at home promote holiness or defilement? Why would we bring any unclean thing into our home or churches? These places should be bastions of purity where righteousness dwells, not squalors of rebellion.

THE PRIESTHOOD OF BELIEVERS IN PAUL

Temple and sexual immorality at Corinth. The church at Corinth was rife with moral issues and internal strife. The Corinthians struggled mightily with living as believers in the midst of the pagan culture of a bustling metropolis. Gordon Fee famously quipped, "Although they were the Christian church in Corinth, an inordinate amount of Corinth was yet in them."[5] In 2 Corinthians 6 Paul admonishes the church to "not be yoked together with unbelievers" (2 Corinthians 6:14). He is probably speaking here of sexual union between believers and unbelievers. What makes the apostle's imperative noteworthy is how he supports his argument: "What agreement is there between the temple of God and idols? For *we are the temple of the living God*" (2 Corinthians 6:16). The Corinthians must avoid sexual relationships with unbelievers *because*, as believers, they are part of God's end-time temple.

Paul then puts together a string of several Old Testament texts in 2 Corinthians 6:16-18: Leviticus 26:11-12; 2 Samuel 7:14; Ezekiel 11:17; 20:34, 41; 37:27; Isaiah 43:6; 49:22; 52:11; 60:4. These Old Testament passages refer to God's promise to redeem Israel from captivity and anticipate the

---

[5]Gordon D. Fee, *The First Epistle to the Corinthians*, NICNT (Grand Rapids: Eerdmans, 1987), 4.

rebuilding of the temple in Jerusalem. As Paul applies these passages to the church, the Corinthian believers must embrace their identity as redeemed Israel and the end-time temple of God. The arrival of God's presence, though, carries with it incredible priestly responsibilities. Consider how careful the Israelite priests maintained the tabernacle and temple. The law of Moses outlined in remarkable detail how the various parts of the temple were to be purified and set apart for God's presence. Israel, too, was to maintain perfect holiness through the sacrificial system as the temple was in their midst. A perfect God demands a perfect people. But Paul, by citing all those Old Testament promises, argues that the believers in Corinth, Gentiles nonetheless, are the true temple! The glory of God that occupied the mobile tabernacle and Solomon's temple was a shadow of what fills the Corinthians.

The Corinthians must embrace their identity as priests who worship in God's temple and maintain its purity. One tangible way in which they function as priests is to rid themselves of all sexual impurity. As the Israelites were encamped at Sinai and made preparations to enter the Promised Land and fight the Canaanites, God charged the Levites to guard his tabernacle: "Anyone else who approaches it [the tabernacle] is to be *put to death*. The Israelites are to set up their tents by divisions, each of them in their own camp under their standard. The Levites, however, are to set up their tents around the tabernacle of the covenant law *so that my wrath will not fall on the Israelite community*" (Numbers 1:51-53). The priests of Israel were deemed guardians of God's holiness, responsible for keeping the dwelling place of God free from contamination. God's presence is not to be trifled with, as Victor Hamilton rightly exclaims: "An enemy can wipe them [the Israelites] out, but so can God's wrath!"[6] In the same way, all believers are end-time priests who must preserve the holiness of God's temple by guarding their hearts from sin and wickedness. Are our hearts filled with lust and sexual impurity? Or are they committed to Christ and our spouses?

A growing temple. The book of Ephesians has much to say about how Jews and Gentiles find complete equality in Christ and about their responsibility to mediate God's glory to the nations. Paul explains that before faith in Christ,

---

[6]Victor P. Hamilton, *Handbook on the Pentateuch*, 2nd ed. (Grand Rapids: Baker Academic, 2005), 307.

Gentiles were "separate from Christ, excluded from citizenship in Israel and foreigners to the covenants of the promise, without hope and without God in the world" (Ephesians 2:12). But because of Christ's work, Gentiles are now able to participate fully in the covenant community through faith. The cross restores humanity's relationship to God (Ephesians 2:1-10) and provides the means for Gentiles to become part of true Israel (Ephesians 2:11-18). Christ took both Jews and Gentiles and "destroyed the barrier" between them (Ephesians 2:14, 17). He has abolished the national laws contained in the old covenant that divided Jews from Gentiles. Gentiles no longer need to apply the external customs of Israel's laws to become true Israelites.

The last bit of Ephesians 2 fits naturally within the Gentiles' playing a significant part within the establishment of true Israel in the new age (Ephesians 2:19-22). In Christ, the Gentiles are "members of his [God's] household, built on the foundation of the apostles and prophets, with Christ Jesus himself as the chief cornerstone" (Ephesians 2:19-20). Since Christ is the true temple, or the "chief cornerstone," the church is constructed on him and likewise deemed the true temple of God. The entire structure is considered a "holy sanctuary" that "grows" (Ephesians 2:21 HCSB). The church, as a growing temple, fulfills God's original intention that his glory would eventually fill the earth.

Adam and Eve were created in God's image so that they might mirror his attributes on the earth and that they might fill every inch of the world with his glory. We see their original goal being realized in Ephesians 2. The church is the restored people of God that houses the glory of God. According to Ephesians 2:15, God created a "new man" out of Jews and Gentiles (NASB). The wording here suggests that the church, composed of Jews and Gentiles, is a corporate last Adam figure. The outward national regulations that were part of the Mosaic covenant prevented Jews and Gentiles from becoming a unified, collective Adam. But now that Christ has come and fulfilled those laws, there is no longer any need for their continuance. God's people are finally in a position to pursue deep unity with one another and become a light to the nations. God's glory is beginning to burst forth on the earth, just like he promised it would, and the church is tasked with continuing the promulgation of it. The reason why the church continues to "grow" into the temple is because there's still work to be done.

THE PRIESTHOOD OF BELIEVERS IN 1 PETER

Much of what is found in Ephesians 2 can also be discerned in 1 Peter 2. Christ is described in like manner as a "living Stone," who was "rejected" by the world yet deemed "precious" to God (1 Peter 2:4; cf. Psalm 118:22). As a faithful priest, Christ began the process of constructing the new, cosmic temple and filling it with God's glory. He is the beginning and the foundation stone of the new cosmic temple. Just as Christ is the living Stone, so too his followers are considered little living stones. The church, as a result of Christ's work, is to be conceived as a "spiritual house" in which the presence of God dwells (1 Peter 2:5).

Peter continues his train of thought by labeling the church as a "holy priesthood, offering spiritual sacrifices" (1 Peter 2:5). Notice how Peter claims that the church enjoys two distinct realities: the church as a temple and the church as a corporate priest. Priests serve in the temple and for the people of Israel so that God may dwell in their midst. Here Peter brings both spiritual realities together. Christians enjoy God's heavenly presence motivating them to offer up their lives as a spiritual sacrifice back to God (see Romans 12:1; Hebrews 13:15).

Heaping up one Old Testament quotation after another, Peter then quotes a combination of three texts: Exodus 19:6; Isaiah 43:20-21; and Hosea 2:23. The first quotation ("a chosen people") originates from Isaiah 43:20-21:

> The wild animals honor me,
>> the jackals and the owls,
> because I provide water in the wilderness
>> and streams in the wasteland,
> to give drink *to my people, my chosen,*
>> the people I formed for myself,
>> that they may proclaim my praise.

The thrust of the Old Testament context there is that the Lord will bring his people out of Babylonian exile (cf. Isaiah 65:17). By applying this phrase from Isaiah 43 to the congregations in Asia Minor, Peter is claiming that the church is part of the new creation, the restored people of God.

Second, Peter quotes from Exodus 19 when he uses the phrase "a royal priesthood, a holy nation" (1 Peter 2:9). I noted in chapter three that Exodus 19:6

states that *if* Israel perfectly obeys God's law, then the nation will be a "kingdom of priests." Perfect obedience to God's law results in service to the nations. As priests mediate God's presence to the Israelites, so too the nation of Israel was to mediate God's presence to the surrounding nations. But Israel failed to keep God's original commission of Genesis 1:28. Instead of mediating God's presence to the nations, Israel worshiped and bowed down to idols. Israel should have transformed into the perfected image of God through obeying his law, but they were transformed into the image of the false gods of the nations through disobedience. But Christ's perfect, faithful life created a new humanity, a people group that is fashioned into his perfected image.

Pay careful attention to Peter's wording here: "You *are* a chosen people, a royal priesthood, a holy nation," whereas Exodus 19:5-6 states, "Now *if* you obey me fully and keep my covenant, *then* out of all nations you will be my treasured possession. . . . *You will be* for me a kingdom of priests and a holy nation." Exodus 19:5-6 is conditional, while 1 Peter 2:9 is a statement of reality. Christ has met the condition of Exodus 19:5, so now the church rightfully inherits their identity as a "royal priesthood." This quotation of Exodus 19:6 underscores the missional nature of the church. The success of Christ's faithful life fuels the church's desire to reach the lost and gives them the greatest message of all—intimacy with their Creator.

THE PRIESTHOOD OF BELIEVERS IN HEBREWS

No other book in the New Testament dedicates so much attention to the nature of Christ's superior priestly office and its benefits for believers than the letter to the Hebrews. Christ is a better sacrifice, a better high priest, a better mediator, a better temple. As tempting as it was for the audience of Hebrews, why turn back to the old covenant when Christ is so much better? What the old covenant contained in part, Christ contains in full.

The old covenant regulations were unable to "perfect" the Israelites (Hebrews 10:1). That is, the sacrifices did not grant Israelites access to God's full presence. Quite simply, "It is impossible for the blood of bulls and goats to take away sins" (Hebrews 10:4). Believers are only cleansed "through the sacrifice of the body of Jesus Christ once for all" (Hebrews 10:10). Only through Christ's perfect obedience is he qualified to be an atoning sacrifice for sin.

The second half of Hebrews 10, the fourth warning passage of the book (Hebrews 10:19-39), continues to highlight the priestly status of all believers. Christ is the "great priest" (Hebrews 10:21), and believers participate in his priestly status. Believers have begun to have access to God's heavenly temple through Christ's continual work as a priestly mediator (Hebrews 10:19-21), so they must "draw near to God with a sincere heart and with the full assurance that faith brings" (Hebrews 10:22a). Identification with Christ in the heavenly temple inevitably propels believers to rid themselves of sin and pursue righteousness (Hebrews 10:22b-26).

As strange as it might seem, believers have begun to experience heaven, at least positionally, through the person of Christ. The author of Hebrews is thinking along these lines when he states,

> You have not come to a mountain [Sinai] that can be touched and that is burning with fire; to darkness, gloom and storm. . . .
> But you have come to Mount Zion, to the city of the living God, *the heavenly Jerusalem*. (Hebrews 12:18, 22)

Those united to Christ have already entered the heavenly holy of holies through their forerunner, Jesus (Hebrews 10:19-22; 4:14-16), resulting in their identification with "Mount Zion . . . the heavenly Jerusalem" (Hebrews 12:22; cf. Galatians 4:26; Revelation 21–22). Through faith in Christ (Hebrews 12:25-27), believers have begun to experience the immeasurable spiritual realities that the Old Testament saints longed for. As marvelous as it was for the high priest to enter the holy of holies once a year on behalf of the Israelites and catch a glimmer of God's presence, New Testament believers experience God's presence in a far more glorious way.

THE PRIESTHOOD OF BELIEVERS IN REVELATION

The book of Revelation accents the priesthood of all believers perhaps more than any other book in the New Testament. Revelation claims that the faithful church on earth is represented in the heavenly temple and before the throne of God. It is true that the church is the temple of God and that his presence dwells in us, but his *full* presence still resides in his heavenly temple, where the deceased saints gather with the angels in worship. In the incarnation Christ irreversibly opened up access to God's heavenly presence. He bridged the heavenly and earthly realities. Through Christ's work, God's presence in heaven extends down to earth, allowing the church to enjoy his glory. To use a sci-fi metaphor, Christ is the portal between these two locations. The physical and spiritual dimensions now intersect with one another.

We see glimmers of this reality in Revelation 5:8-10:

> And when he had taken it, the four living creatures and *the twenty-four elders* fell down before the Lamb. Each one had a harp and they were holding golden bowls full of incense, *which are the prayers of God's people.* And they sang a new song, saying:

> "You are worthy to take the scroll
>> and to open its seals,
> because you were slain,
>> and with your blood you purchased for God
>> persons from every tribe and language and people and nation.
> You have made them to *be a kingdom and priests* to serve our God,
>> and they will reign on the earth." (cf. Revelation 4:4-11)

Identifying the twenty-four elders sitting on heavenly thrones in Revelation 4:4 and Revelation 5:8 has been the subject of much debate. The most satisfying view identifies them as angelic representatives of the people of God throughout the ages. They are angels who represent the covenant community in the Old and New Testaments—twelve for the people of God under the old covenant (the twelve patriarchs) and twelve for those under the new covenant (the twelve apostles).[7] What's critical, though, is how they are functioning here in Revelation 5:8: "Each one had a harp and they were holding golden bowls full of incense, *which are the prayers of God's people.*" These twenty-four angels serve the church in a priestly capacity before the throne. Just as the priests offered up incense to God in the temple (Exodus 30:7-8), so too the angels offer up the incense of the prayers of God's people on earth. The point is that the suffering church, though on earth, is represented in heaven before the throne. Through angelic representation, believers on earth participate in

---

[7]Grant R. Osborne, *Revelation*, BECNT (Grand Rapids: Baker Academic, 2002), 229.

heavenly worship before God. When we worship and extol the Lord, the angels worship and extol the Lord. Our worship is their worship.

In Revelation 5:10 we glean further insight into the nature of our identity as priests. The twenty-four angels continue to praise Christ for his work of redemption in making the church "to be a kingdom and priests to serve our God." Once again, we have an allusion to Exodus 19:6, where Moses expresses God's desire that Israel be a "kingdom of priests." John here claims that the church is fulfilling God's ultimate intention that his people rule over his creation and enjoy his glory forever.

CONCLUSION AND APPLICATION

The descent of the Spirit at Pentecost filled God's people with his glorious presence, empowering them to live holy lives, enjoy God's glory, and proclaim the gospel to the ends of the earth. Our rich identity as end-time priests is immensely practical on many levels. Believers should embrace the reality that the church is fundamentally a community of priests enjoying God's presence in their midst. Karen Jobes rightly argues, "The Christian church is not primarily a social organization but the new temple where the transformed lives of believers are offered as sacrifice to the glory of God."[8] Our lives must be characterized by service to God and one another.

Though our culture tells us otherwise, we do not exist to glorify and honor ourselves but to offer up praise to God. Recall that Adam and Eve were to image God and bring him glory in all their thoughts and actions by depending solely on him. They sinned when they attempted to come out from their reliance on him. Dependence on God is central to who we are as believers. Our culture seeks to find strength and power from within us, whereas the Bible instructs us to find strength in what Christ has achieved on our behalf. God empowers us in Christ when we depend on him.

As priests the church should consciously view itself as the means by which God will fill the earth with the

> knowledge of the glory of the Lord,
> as the waters cover the sea. (Habakkuk 2:14)

---

[8]Karen H. Jobes, *1 Peter*, BECNT (Grand Rapids: Baker Academic, 2005), 149.

We are to mediate God's glory to our family, our neighbors, our coworkers, and the nations. If God's glory is our supreme joy, then how can we keep it to ourselves? Will we not want to share the redemption we enjoy with others? The book of Numbers highlights the role of priests as buffers between God's awesome presence and the Israelites. According to Numbers 16:48, Aaron prevented God's wrath from wiping out the entire Israelite community because of their rebellion: "He [Aaron] stood between the living and the dead, and the plague stopped" (cf. Numbers 8:19). The principle we glean is that priests procure the safety of humanity by offering up acceptable service to God. Believers must be mindful of the lost and consciously view themselves as those who stand in the gap between God's wrath and his life-giving presence.

RECOMMENDED READING

Alexander, T. Desmond. *From Eden to the New Jerusalem: An Introduction to Biblical Theology*. Grand Rapids: Kregel, 2009.

Ellingworth, P. "Priests." In *New Dictionary of Biblical Theology*, edited by T. Desmond Alexander, Brian S. Rosner, D. A. Carson, and Graeme Goldsworthy, 696-701. Downers Grove, IL: InterVarsity Press, 2000.

Malone, Andrew S. *God's Mediators: A Biblical Theology of Priesthood*. NSBT 43. Downers Grove, IL: IVP Academic, 2017.

Chapter Ten

THE CHURCH AS PROPHETS

WE NOW TURN to our third and final dimension of believers being the image of God—the church as a collective prophet. A prophet is someone who hears God's word, speaks on behalf of him to his people, and embodies his truth. Adam and Eve received God's law and were charged with meditating on it and teaching it to their children (Genesis 1:28; 2:16-17). But they failed. The same expectation was repeated at Sinai, where God gave the nation of Israel his perfect law (Exodus 20–31). Again, they failed. So God sent his Son to obey and fulfill his law and embody the divine truth on earth. At every point in his life, Jesus remained steadfast and faithful to the law and the Father's will. The success of Jesus as the perfect prophet created a new humanity, the eschatological Israel, to embody God's law and communicate it to others.

THE PROPHETIC MINISTRY OF BELIEVERS
IN THE GOSPELS AND ACTS

The prophetic commissioning of the disciples. The prophetic dimension of the disciples and the followers of Jesus comes to the forefront in the book of Acts, but we can catch a few glimmers of it in the Gospels. The appointment of the twelve disciples in Matthew 10 reveals the outward dimension of the prophetic office (cf. Luke 10:1-16). The twelve disciples, symbolizing the restored twelve tribes of Israel, are to target initially the "lost sheep of Israel" (Matthew 10:5-15) and then expand their mission to the surrounding nations (Matthew 10:17-42; cf. Matthew 28:19-20). Israel's failure to do so in the Old Testament anticipates the success of true Israel in the New Testament.

In Matthew's account, the commissioning of the twelve disciples is accompanied with sobering expectations:

> Be on your guard; you will be handed over to the local councils and be flogged in the synagogues. On my account you will be brought before governors and kings as *witnesses* to them and to the Gentiles. But when they arrest you, do not worry about what to say or how to say it. At that time *you will be given what to say, for it will not be you speaking, but the Spirit of your Father speaking through you.* (Matthew 10:17-20; cf. Mark 13:9)

We briefly looked at the commissioning of the disciples in chapter eight, but we will again turn our attention to it here as it relates to the prophetic witness of the church.

Jesus assures the disciples here in Matthew 10 that they will follow in his footsteps and eventually be rejected by their own people. The disciples must gain comfort knowing that the Spirit will give them insight and the right words to say to their captors (cf. John 15:26-27). The disciples will function as the mouthpiece of God to the world and especially to their adversaries. The disciples of Jesus will be successful in reaching the nations, yet their success comes with a steep price tag—rejection by their own Jewish community and the empire.

At the end of the commission, Jesus promises the disciples that they represent him in their ministry efforts, just as he represents the Father (Matthew 10:40). The words of the disciples are the very words of Jesus, and the words of Jesus are the words of God. Matthew 10:41 discloses the operating principle: "Whoever welcomes a prophet as a prophet will receive a prophet's reward." Here the disciples are viewed as standing in the tradition of Old Testament prophets who herald God's message to the people (cf. Matthew 5:12). If the audience believes the message of the disciples, the audience "will receive . . . a reward," that is, eternal life.

The gospel "growing" and "multiplying" in Acts. Genesis 1:28, as we've seen, is a critical passage for understanding the nature of the people of God—his expectations for humanity and what he desires for all of creation. The book of Acts weaves Genesis 1:28 into the fabric of its narrative, underscoring the fulfillment of God's long-awaited goal. In Genesis 1:28, Adam and Eve were commanded to "multiply," while in Acts the gospel "multiplies" or "grows." The distinction is critical. True multiplication of the people of God is more than simply bearing children; it is the transfer of God's image to one's descendants. Adam bore a son "in his own likeness, in his own image" (Genesis 5:3) because he passed along more than physical traits to Seth. Though Cain and Seth are physical descendants of Adam, only one is a true, spiritual descendant of Adam.

The book of Acts is attuned to the spiritual dimension of Genesis 1:28 and the growth of the people of God. For example, Acts 6:7 reads, "And the word of God continued to *increase*, and the number of the disciples *multiplied* greatly in Jerusalem" (ESV). The unique wording alludes to Genesis 1:28, where Adam and Eve are to "Be *fruitful* and *multiply*, and *fill* the earth, and subdue it; and rule over the fish of the sea and over the birds of the sky and over every living thing that moves on the earth" (NASB). The book of Acts picks up on this language of "growing" and "multiplying" but at strategic junctures within the narrative to mark key events during the first decades of the early church (Acts 6:7; 9:31; 12:24; 16:5; 19:20).[1] The apostles, as prophets, faithfully proclaimed the gospel to Israel and the nations without fear or loss of life.

The growth of the gospel in Acts, though, exceeds human expectations. The expansion of the gospel accelerates through the persecution and suffering of God's people. Just as the curse in Genesis 3:16 promises that Eve will multiply through severe pains in childbearing, so too the church multiplies in the face of persecution in the book of Acts. Looks can be deceiving. The people of God may appear on the outside to be weak and insignificant. But that's not how God views either his people or the spread of the gospel. When all hope appears lost and the world is doing its worst to us, that's when the message of Christ shines its brightest.

---

[1]David G. Peterson, *The Acts of the Apostles*, PNTC (Grand Rapids: Eerdmans, 2009), 32-34.

The reversal of Babel at Pentecost. God's intention has always been to dwell with all of humanity. Each person, regardless of race or ethnicity, is created in the image of God, so we are all fashioned to enjoy his presence. The tower of Babel splintered humanity and drove a wedge between the various people groups (Genesis 11:1-9), but Abraham is promised that his descendants will bless all peoples on earth (Genesis 12:3; 18:18). One word could describe the social dimension of the Old Testament—division. Yet division will not prevail. The Old Testament prophets predicted that people groups would live in harmony in the end time (e.g., Isaiah 2:3; 56:3-8; Zechariah 2:11; 8:20-23).

Now that Christ has come, all of creation and humanity has found its unity in Christ. At Pentecost Babel has been reversed. Luke's presentation of the diaspora Jews at Pentecost in Acts 2:9-11 alludes to the Table of Nations in Genesis 10. According to Genesis 10, Noah's sons multiplied into the seventy nations, spreading out over various regions in Mesopotamia. Genesis 11:1 states that the whole earth had "one language and a common speech." A large number of people that represented the seventy nations decided to construct a city and a "tower that reaches to the heavens." The point of this tower, they said, was to "make a name for ourselves; otherwise we will be scattered over the face of the whole earth" (Genesis 11:4). This purpose is diametrically opposed to Genesis 1:28. Indeed, the tower of Babel contrasts Eden and Sinai. "Babel is not only the antithesis of the holy city that God desires to build upon the earth, but it is also its great rival and opponent."[2] Instead of worshiping the Lord at a divinely sanctioned sanctuary (Eden/Sinai), humanity constructs an idolatrous temple at Babel to worship themselves. In Genesis 1, God commanded Adam and Eve to spread God's glory to the ends of the earth, but here in Genesis 11 humanity assembles together. Instead of making a name for God, humanity makes a name for itself (Genesis 11:4). By confusing their language, God prevents humanity from functioning as one and from achieving their selfish inclinations and ambitions. Humanity is permanently divided—separated by various languages.

---

[2]T. Desmond Alexander, *The City of God and the Goal of Creation*, Short Studies in Biblical Theology (Wheaton, IL: Crossway, 2018), 27.

God's judgment at Babel is finally reversed at Pentecost: representatives from the scattered nations find true harmony by the power of the Spirit in Jerusalem (cf. Luke 10). These Israelites who gathered in Jerusalem to celebrate Pentecost now function as prophets by bearing witness to Jesus' death, resurrection, and ascension to the heavenly throne to reign as cosmic king (see Acts 1:8).

The list of diaspora Jews in Acts 2:9-11 betrays an intentional geographic order. Beginning with those living in the East and then moving counterclockwise, Luke demonstrates that God, at Pentecost, is restoring diaspora Jews with Jerusalem functioning as the center. The regathered people of Israel will faithfully testify to the risen Lord, beginning in Jerusalem, and will then fan out to the "ends of the earth."

A central tenant of fulfilling the prophetic dimension of being created in God's image is to communicate God's word to others, especially our relatives. Sharing the gospel with those who know us intimately is difficult. They know our failings; they know our weaknesses; they've seen the worst in us. Unfortunately, I find it easier to talk about Christ with a complete stranger than with a close neighbor.

THE PROPHETIC MINISTRY OF BELIEVERS IN PAUL

Cosmic testimony. The prophetic role of the church is prominently on display in Paul's letter to the Ephesians, especially in how it's bound up with the cosmos. This is an often neglected yet important dimension of imaging God on earth, so I will spend a bit of space developing it. The word *mystery* is a hot-button issue in the New Testament, and it features prominently in Ephesians. Briefly, the word *mystery* refers to a revelation that was generally hidden in the Old Testament but has now been fully revealed in the New Testament. Paul's use of the word in Ephesians entails three concentric themes, all of which pertain to unity. In Ephesians 1, the cosmic mystery concerns the unification of all things in Christ. Ephesians 3 encompasses an ethnic mystery—the manner in which Jews and Gentiles are united in Christ. Finally, in Ephesians 5, the marital mystery is discussed. The unity between a husband and wife correlates to that between Christ and the church. It is Paul's "ethnic" mystery that we are particularly interested in.

After discussing Christ's cosmic rule and the subsequent unity of all things, Paul continues the theme of unity in Ephesians 2–3 but with an eye on unity between people groups. Just as all things are united in Christ, so Jews and Gentiles are joined together in him. We therefore ought to view the use of mystery in Ephesians 3 as deeply rooted in the cosmic mystery of Ephesians 1. In Ephesians 3, the apostle articulates *how* Gentiles participate in true Israel— by faith. In the Old Testament and Judaism, Gentiles convert and become full-fledged Jewish proselytes by taking on the yoke of the law, obeying the laws of the sacrificial system and so on.

Paul's gospel claims that Gentile entrance into Israel is strictly by faith, apart from identifying with any of Israel's laws that formerly identified people as Israelites. He succinctly explains, "This mystery is that through the gospel the Gentiles are heirs together with Israel, members together of one body, and sharers together in the promise in Christ Jesus" (Ephesians 3:6). Simply put, the mystery comprises how Gentiles become true Israelites without taking on the external markers of the old covenant. The result of Paul's teaching is complete unity between two previously estranged people groups— Jews and Gentiles. Now that Christ has come, these two people groups are in complete unity with one another.

Perhaps one of the reasons why Paul highlights Christian unity in Ephesians lies in the Old Testament conception of unity or lack thereof. Paul claims that the gospel, particularly the unity between Jews and Gentiles, testifies to "rulers and authorities" (Ephesians 3:10). The notoriously difficult expression "rulers and authorities" probably refers to the invisible, demonic forces that are fused with our physical world. The church is therefore the vehicle for proclaiming unity to the demonic forces. What is the relationship between unity and angels?

According to the Old Testament (and Second Temple Judaism), God appointed angels to rule over the nations on his behalf (Genesis 11). We see this phenomenon in Deuteronomy 32:8:

> When the Most High gave to the nations their inheritance,
>   when he divided mankind,
> he fixed the borders of the peoples
>   *according to the number of the sons of God.* (ESV)

The last phrase of this verse is notoriously difficult to pin down, and many translations render the last phrase as "sons of Israel" (NIV, NASB, HCSB). But the Septuagint (the Greek translation of the Old Testament) is explicit: "according to the number of the angels of God" (see NLT). These angelic overseers were to maintain separation between the various people groups. Israel, however, did not have an intermediary acting on behalf of God.[3] God had an intimate relationship with Israel and did not require one. Instead of ruling well on God's behalf, corrupt angels usurped their God-given authority and sought to become powerful by attempting to be the source of power and authority (Psalm 82; cf. Deuteronomy 4:19; Judges 11:24; Daniel 10:13, 20; Acts 17:26).

The Old Testament conception of (dis)unity has a direct bearing on the book of Ephesians, especially Paul's articulation of "rulers and authorities" in Ephesians 3:10. He feels compelled to proclaim this mystery "to the rulers and authorities in the heavenly realms" (Ephesians 3:10). But notice how the church plays a direct role in the proclamation of the mystery: "that now, *through the church*, the manifold wisdom of God [i.e., the mystery] should be made known to the rulers and authorities" (Ephesians 3:10). Paul preaches the mystery to the church, who in turn proclaim it to the world and the "rulers and authorities."

Why is Paul so concerned that the church use its prophetic role with the demonic forces? The answer probably lies in the Old Testament understanding of angels and their role in maintaining separation between the nations. The seventy nations were represented by seventy angels. Angels, therefore, came to symbolize the lack of unity between the nations.

If the Old Testament views the nations as being divided, the New Testament says just the opposite. In Christ all nations find unity and total equality (Acts 2:1-41). Therefore, Paul tells the church at Ephesus to remain unified in order to testify to the inimical forces that God has now reversed his decree at Babel. Division and fracture are characteristic of the "ages past" (Ephesians 3:9; cf. Galatians 3:26-29). Instead of being splintered according to

---

[3]See Daniel Block, *The Gods of the Nations: Studies in Ancient Near Eastern National Theology*, 2nd ed. (Grand Rapids: Baker Academic, 2000), 32; G. B. Caird, *New Testament Theology*, ed. L. D. Hurst (Oxford: Clarendon, 1995), 102-3.

people groups, the church constitutes the restored people of God from every nation. Unity is now emblematic of the new age.

When viewed from this angle, the prophetic ministry of the church is staggering. First, we must embody robust unity in all our actions. We are compelled to live according to the new age, the age of unity in Christ. The practical implications of this truth run deep. Do we disparage people from another race? Do we do the same to the poor or those from a different social class? If we do, we are reverting to the old age, the age of division and fracture. If, though, we view everyone through the lens of the new age, the age of unity, all stand equal at the foot of the cross, and we treat one another accordingly. Do we cause division in our church? Do we gossip or sow seeds of discord among the congregation? It may seem innocuous at first, but gossip or slander will begin to take root, and division will inevitably result. Do our homes reflect the old age? Do we quarrel with our spouses and children? Is divorce an option?

Second, we must recognize that our actions are prophetic, reverberating throughout the cosmos. Actions are often louder than words. When we as Christians behave in this divisive manner, we are prophetically declaring to the demons that they still hold sway and that the gospel of unity makes little or no difference in our daily lives. But when Christians maintain unity at home, within our congregations, and out in the community, we are trumpeting the gospel and declaring to the angels that our lives are emblematic of the new age.

On guard. In chapter four I mentioned the arrival of a latter-day antagonist who will infiltrate the covenant community and deceive many within it. As an anti-prophet, this figure will use his winsome personality to sway unstable people. His deception results in some within the community forsaking the holy covenant (Daniel 11:30). His influence through flattery also extends to those "who have violated the covenant" to become even more godless (Daniel 11:32), to compromise, and to foster deception and further compromise among others. Daniel 11:34 reveals that "many who are not sincere will join them [the faithful]." These Israelites only have a veneer of faith. They claim to be faithful to God's law, but are, in reality, unfaithful.

The New Testament latches on to texts such as Daniel 11 and applies them to what's transpiring in the first century. Indeed, one of the more prominent themes running throughout the New Testament is the emphasis on false teaching. At the Olivet Discourse, Jesus discusses end-time opponents of Israel using language from the book of Daniel: "Many will come in my name, claiming, 'I am the Messiah,' and will deceive many" (Matthew 24:5). "And many false prophets will appear and deceive many people" (Matthew 24:11; cf. Matthew 24:23-26). Jesus envisions an antichrist figure(s) who will deceive Israel preceding the destruction of the temple in AD 70. His influence will be a sign that Israel's destruction is near. In Matthew 24:5, the oppressor will be characterized by deception, claiming to be "the Messiah" and, therefore, upsetting the faith of many.

In 2 Thessalonians Paul corrects the Thessalonian church's confusion over the second coming of Christ. He makes it clear that Christ's second coming has not yet occurred, since that day will be preceded by two events: "apostasy" and the unveiling of the "man of lawlessness" (2 Thessalonians 2:3 NASB). Paul claims in 2 Thessalonians 2:3 that Daniel's "man of lawlessness" has not yet arrived on the scene, but, alarmingly, there is a sense in which the end-time oppressor is already on the scene. This suggestion explains the language in 2 Thessalonians 2:7: "The *mystery* of lawlessness is already at work" (NASB). Second Thessalonians 2:7 is not a general form of wickedness and persecution but a specific end-time deception and persecution that ought to be attributed to the church's end-time antagonist. Paul employs "mystery" here in 2 Thessalonians 2:7 to describe a unique situation with startling ramifications: according to Daniel, the end-time persecutor will appear to the covenant community in his full bodily presence in the future, yet Paul argues that the antagonist is nevertheless "already at work" in the community.

John's words in 1 John 2:18 are even more striking: "Dear children, this is the last hour; and as you have heard that the antichrist is coming, *even now many antichrists have come.* This is how we know it is the last hour." The church is to be on high alert for false teaching, so it must embrace the apostolic message of the gospel and its implications for daily living.

TO PROPHESY OR NOT TO PROPHESY

Up to this point, I have argued that every believer is, because of their union with Christ, an end-time king, priest, and prophet. Does it follow, then, that Christians should expect the same prophetic gifts or charisms of the Spirit to continue today? That is, do the gifts of the Spirit, such as "tongues," "prophecy," and "miraculous powers," continue today? This is a difficult subject, and scholars debate this issue with great vigor.

There are many permutations of the various views, but I will restrict myself to relaying three general camps. First, scholars within the charismatic tradition argue that spiritual gifts are essential for worship in the local church and in the Christian life. The second view is a bit more tempered. Some scholars advocate the continuation of spiritual gifts but not the "second blessing" of the Spirit in the Christian life. The third view is convinced that the spiritual gifts, though an important part of the establishment of the early church in the first century, have ceased operating today.

Representing a subset of the third view, Vern Poythress argues that Christ is the supreme king, priest, and prophet. The apostles, though they are not as pristinely and perfectly kings, priests, and prophets as Christ, nevertheless embody all three offices in a unique way. Believers today, on account of their identity in Christ, are still kings, priests, and prophets, but they are less so than Christ and the apostles. He illustrates this idea in figure 10.1.[4]

The advantage of this view advocated by Poythress is that it retains the threefold office of believers yet maintains distinctions between Christ and the apostles and between the apostles and believers today. Poythress describes the gifts of today as "analogous" to the apostolic gifts and thus "fallible."[5]

We can apply this keen insight to our daily lives in many ways. Pastors and teachers, as they employ their prophetic office, can be confident that the Spirit is working in their lives to explain and make known the oracles of God to their congregations. Christ has succeeded as a faithful prophet, so believers today are empowered to meditate on God's law, adhere to it, and herald it to others.

---

[4]Vern Poythress, *What Are Spiritual Gifts?* (Phillipsburg, NJ: P&R, 2010), 14. Adapted with permission.
[5]Poythress, *What Are Spiritual Gifts*, 37.

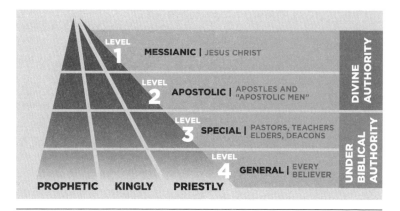

Figure 10.1

CONCLUSION AND APPLICATION

One of the fundamental reasons why Adam and Eve sinned in the garden was their lack of meditation and careful handling of God's law. The serpent manipulated God's word in Genesis 3:1: "Did God really say, 'You must not eat from any tree in the garden'?" (Genesis 3:1). God did not command that. Adam and Eve were "free to eat from any tree in the garden" (Genesis 2:16) but not from the tree of the knowledge of good and evil. Eve's response to the temptation is also illuminating: "We may eat fruit from the trees in the garden, but God did say, 'You must not eat fruit from the tree that is in the middle of the garden, and you must not touch it, or you will die'" (Genesis 3:2-3). God didn't say anything about not touching the fruit. God also said that they would "certainly die" (Genesis 2:17), whereas Eve softens the curse when she claims that she would simply "die" (Genesis 3:3). So we learn that the serpent tweaked God's law just enough to tempt Eve. The same could be said today. When Satan tempts us, it's typically not an outright lie; rather, Satan uses subtlety to ensnare. He is called an angel of light for a reason (2 Corinthians 11:14). But appearances are often deceiving. We need to teach more of the Bible at home and in our local churches, not less.

RECOMMENDED READING

Clowney, Edmund. *Preaching Christ in All of Scripture*. Wheaton, IL: Crossway, 2003.

Griffiths, Jonathan. *Preaching in the New Testament: An Exegetical and Biblical-Theological Study*. NSBT 42. Downers Grove, IL: IVP Academic, 2017.

Johnson, Dennis E. *Him We Proclaim: Preaching Christ from All the Scriptures*. Phillipsburg: P&R, 2007.

Chapter Eleven

THE CHURCH IN
THE NEW CREATION

I AM OFTEN ASKED what heaven will be like. Will we float in the clouds strumming harps? Will our family members recognize us? Will our pets be there? In some sense, questions such as these are a bit odd. The biblical conception of heaven and the afterlife is far more robust and all-encompassing than what we often imagine. My final chapter in this project will primarily focus on the believers' full restoration in the image of God. What began in Christ in his first coming is completed in the new heavens and earth at his second coming.

Before exploring how Revelation contributes to our understanding of being fully restored in the divine image, though, I will first consider its attention to the "anti-image" and the "anti–people of God" and how those realities are a manifestation of the anti-Trinity. We've seen how the Old Testament anticipates the arrival of an anti-image, who will abuse the three offices of king, priest, and prophet. I even noted the arrival of the corporate nature of the anti-image in 2 Thessalonians 2. That is, there is a sense in which the antichrist began to infiltrate the church in the first century but only through inspiring his false teachers (1 John 2:18). Just as we represent Christ on the earth, so the false teachers represent the antichrist. The book of Revelation ramps up the discussion of the anti–people of God and starkly contrasts them with the church. The result of this investigation should stimulate trust in Christ's work and inflame our passion to bring glory and honor to God alone.

A TALE OF TWO WOMEN

In keeping with the Old Testament, John symbolically depicts the people of God as a woman. We see this sketched in great detail in Revelation 12, where a dragon wages war against the woman who is "clothed with the sun, with the moon under her feet and a crown of twelve stars on her head" (Revelation 12:1; cf. Genesis 37:9). The woman symbolizes the true people of God, "the mother of the promised Seed who would slay the serpent."[1] We discover at the end of Revelation that the woman is also equated with the new Jerusalem (Revelation 21:2, 9).

In Revelation 17 we encounter a second woman—"the great prostitute, who sits by many waters" (Revelation 17:1). The reason why she is labeled a prostitute is because "the kings of the earth committed adultery" with her (Revelation 17:2). The woman, symbolizing the world economic system, has seduced the state to trust her and create an alliance with her. On her forehead she bears the title "Babylon the Great" (Revelation 17:5). She is also bent on imitating the true church. She is "dressed in purple and scarlet, and . . . glittering with gold, precious stones and pearls" (Revelation 17:4; cf. Revelation 18:16). Remarkably, her dress is almost identical to the appearance of the true church depicted in Revelation 21:18-19: "the city of pure gold . . . the foundations of the city walls were decorated with every kind of precious stone." Revelation, therefore, depicts two cities as two women. The true people of God are a faithful bride, that is, the new Jerusalem, whereas the unfaithful are a prostitute, namely, Babylon.

Throughout Revelation the true church executes its threefold office as king, priest, and prophet for the glory of God and the furtherance of the gospel. The true church images God on earth. As kings, the church imitates Christ by spiritually ruling over the world by becoming physically overcome by it (e.g., Revelation 2:7; 5:5; 11:7; 12:11). As priests, the church is depicted as a lampstand that enjoys God's glory and radiates it to a hostile world (Revelation 2:1, 5; cf. 11:4). And as prophets, the church bears witness to God's truth at all costs, just as Christ bore witness (Revelation 1:2, 5, 9; 6:9; 11:3; 12:11).

---

[1]Dennis E. Johnson, *Triumph of the Lamb: A Commentary on Revelation* (Phillipsburg, NJ: P&R), 180.

Juxtaposed with Christ's and the church's faithfulness in their threefold office, the ungodly or the anti–people of God use their threefold office for destruction. The ungodly image themselves on earth for their own glory. As anti-kings, the world wages warfare on God's people through martyrdom and abuse (Revelation 11:7; 13:7). As anti-priests, the world attempts to defile the true temple, the church, and construct its own system of worship (Revelation 2:14; 9:21; 18:3). As anti-prophets, the world speaks lies and generates its own set of laws (Revelation 3:9; 16:13; 19:20).

THE TRINITY AND THE ANTI-TRINITY

A key contribution of the book of Revelation is its penchant for pulling back the curtains and informing God's people of what is taking place on a spiritual level. Looks can be deceiving. When it comes to the nature of God's people and the anti–people of God, Revelation graphically narrates how the triune God energizes and nourishes the true church on earth and how the anti-trinity inspires and sustains the anti–people of God.

The three devilish figures in Revelation 13 (the dragon, the beast from the sea, and the beast from the earth [the false prophet, Revelation 16:13]) are modeled after the Trinity. John alludes to the book of Daniel to describe Satan's alliance with the two grotesque beasts. The description of the first beast (from the sea) in Revelation 13:1-2 resembles the attributes from the four beasts in Daniel 7: ten horns (Revelation 13:1 / Daniel 7:24), appearance like a leopard (Revelation 13:2 / Daniel 7:6). The general sequence of events in Revelation 13 also recalls the events mentioned in Daniel 7 (see table 11.1).

DANIEL 7	REVELATION 13
Four "beasts" emerge from the "sea." (Daniel 7:3)	"Beast" emerges from the "sea." (Revelation 13:1)
The Son of Man receives "authority." (Daniel 7:14)	"Beast" receives "authority" from the dragon. (Revelation 13:2)
The Son of Man is worshiped by the nations. (Daniel 7:14)	The dragon is "worshiped" by the unbelievers. (Revelation 13:3-4)
"Another king" will "speak against" God. (Daniel 7:24-25)	The beast utters "proud words" and "blasphemies." (Revelation 13:5)

Table 11.1

The satanic trinity is bent on imitating the triune God. Where God reveals end-time truth to his people, Satan divulges lies and deception. Where God and the Son of Man possess authority to conquer evil, the beast from the sea enjoys authority to wage war against the church. Eventually, though, the anti-trinity will collapse within itself and is unable to sustain its imitation (Revelation 17:5-18).

Unbelievers will worship the beast by exclaiming "*Who is like the beast? Who can wage war against it?*" (Revelation 13:4). The first rhetorical question is an allusion to Exodus 15:11, where Moses and the Israelites celebrate the Lord's inimitable act of delivering them from the chaotic waters of Red Sea and destroying the Egyptians. Here in Revelation 13:4 unbelievers mimic this adoration, thus underscoring the corrupt worship of a false god.

The reason why we have discussed the anti–people of God and the anti-trinity in Revelation is so that we can adjust our expectations to the Bible's. Imaging God on earth is counterintuitive to the world's ideals. Indeed, it elicits hostility. Though it's tempting to conform to the world, as that would help ensure prosperity and acceptance, we must remain faithful to our calling, to who we are in Christ. He redeemed us so that we might faithfully represent him on the earth and bring him glory in all that we say and do. John's portrayal of the people of God and the people of the world is quite terrifying. In describing the prostitute of Revelation 17, Dennis Johnson remarks, "The vision that opens before John's eyes first paints the harlot Babylon's superficial attractiveness, which explains how she can be alluring not only to pagans but also to Christians."[2] The stakes couldn't be higher. We are fundamentally created to worship, but the question remains: Whom will we adore? Either we worship and glorify the triune God, or we worship false gods and give them and ourselves glory.

THE OLD CREATION AND THE NEW CREATION

Now that I have articulated the nature of the people of God during the overlap of the ages, we can now turn to the nature of God's people in the eternal state, in the new heavens and earth. Genesis 1–2 sets forth the program of God's plan of redemption—God's desire to dwell intimately with creation and his people. We learned in chapter one that God created the cosmos as a gigantic temple with

[2]Johnson, *Triumph of the Lamb*, 242.

the intention of dwelling within it. He made a house for himself, a house that only he can build. But for him to move in and dwell with creation and humanity, Adam and Eve must successfully fulfill God's requirements of being kings, priests, and prophets. Adam and Eve's idolatrous behavior led to their estrangement from God. The presence of God that once nourished Adam and Eve now threatened their very existence. Creation, too, was ravaged in light of the fall. Something had to be done. Only through the obedience and death of Christ, the last Adam and true Israel, can humanity commune with God and creation be restored.

A peculiar thing happened when Christ died and rose from the grave: God began to restore humanity and fashion them in his Son's image, the same image that Adam and Eve were to achieve had they obeyed. The Old Testament, generally speaking, anticipated God's people being restored *fully* at the very end of history (Daniel 12:1-3). However, God did not restore believers fully and completely in the New Testament age. It's true that all believers in Christ are a "new creation" (2 Corinthians 5:17), but they are not fully created anew until Christ returns a second time (1 Corinthians 15:20-28). Only at the general resurrection are believers consummately fashioned in the image of Christ.

Creation, too, began to be restored through the resurrection of Christ. Colossians 1:19-20 states that "God was pleased . . . through him [Christ] to reconcile to himself all things, *whether things on earth or things in heaven*, by making peace through his blood, shed on the cross." The entire cosmos is beginning to be made right through the death and resurrection of Christ. What believers experience through their union with Christ, creation also experiences. When Christ returns, the entire cosmos will experience full-blown restoration.

While it's true that the word *heaven* is indeed biblical, it's not true that we will spend eternity in "heaven." The place we now call heaven is temporary. It is a place where God, his angels, and the deceased saints dwell. But it will not always be like this. Revelation 21–22 clearly affirms that heaven and earth will become one place—the eternal new cosmos.

THE NEW CREATION AS GOD'S TEMPLE

If the original creation was intended to be a massive, cosmic temple, it makes sense then for the new creation to be understood as a cosmic sanctuary. God's original intention to fashion a sanctuary for himself will be fulfilled in its fullness in the new heavens and earth. The Bible begins with God's initial construction of his cosmic temple in Genesis 1–2 and ends with its renovation and consummation in Revelation 21–22. Hardly coincidental.

John's final vision in the book of Revelation can be, like his other visions, puzzling. Notice the first couple of verses: "Then I saw '*a new heaven and a new earth*,' for the first heaven and the first earth had passed away, and there was no longer any sea. *I saw the Holy City, the new Jerusalem*, coming down out of heaven from God, prepared as *a bride beautifully dressed for her husband*" (Revelation 21:1-2).

John gives his audience three images to contemplate—a new cosmos, a city, and a bride. How are all three related to one another? The second half of Revelation 21 answers this question. The "Holy City, the new Jerusalem," is explained in more detail. We learn that the city is a perfectly constructed cube that shines brilliantly (Revelation 21:11-21). Commentators are quick to point out that this heavenly city closely resembles the holy of holies, the innermost room of the temple. The entire cosmos is a gigantic Eden (Revelation 22:1-2).

Circling back to Revelation 21:1, we can see that John's vision of a "new heaven and a new earth" paired with a "Holy City" makes wonderful sense. The new heaven and earth *are* the city! The new cosmos is one massive sanctuary! The third image, the bride, can also be brought to bear on this discussion. According to Revelation 21:9, an angel tells John that he will be shown the "bride, the wife of the Lamb." The angel then proceeds to show him the "Holy City, Jerusalem, coming down out of heaven" (Revelation 21:10). The people of God, who are identified as the bride, are also the city.

The church, figuratively depicted as a city rests on "twelve foundations" who are the "twelve apostles of the Lamb" (Revelation 21:14). Christ and the apostles spearheaded the new, end-time people of God. Built on Christ and the apostles are twelve gates, each of which bear the "names of the twelve tribes of Israel" (Revelation 21:12). While it's tempting to think that "twelve tribes" here refers to the covenant community in the Old Testament, it probably refers to all of God's people spanning both Testaments.[3]

John's final vision therefore concerns the nature of the church in the new creation. He envisions a new cosmos that functions as the dwelling place of

---

[3]See Richard Bauckham, *The Theology of the Book of Revelation* (Cambridge: Cambridge University Press, 1993), 136-40.

God and redeemed humanity. John declares in Revelation 21:22 that he "did not see a temple in the city, because the Lord God Almighty and the Lamb are its temple" (cf. Revelation 21:3). There's no physical structure in the new creation that functions as a temple, since the entire cosmos is one massive sanctuary filled with the glorious presence of the triune God.

PRIESTS IN THE NEW CREATION

Since the bulk of John's last vision concerns the nature of the church in the new creation, we can learn a great deal about what it means to be fully restored in God's image. We will first explore our priestly dimension, a theme that is pronounced in Revelation 22:1-5:

> Then the angel showed me the river of the water of life, as clear as crystal, flowing from the throne of God and of the Lamb down the middle of the great street of the city. On each side of the river stood the tree of life, bearing twelve crops of fruit, yielding its fruit every month. And the leaves of the tree are for the healing of the nations. No longer will there be any curse. The throne of God and of the Lamb will be in the city, and his servants will serve him. They will see his face, *and his name will be on their foreheads.* There will be no more night. They will not need the light of a lamp or the light of the sun, for the Lord God will give them light. *And they will reign for ever and ever.*

In the previous section (Revelation 21:9-27), John primarily sees the church portrayed as an indestructible temple that houses the glory of God. In Revelation 22:1-5, John zeroes in on the reality of the church in the new creation. Notice the spatial progression of the vision, from largest to smallest (see fig. 11.1).

Figure 11.1

The significance is that in Revelation 22:1-5 we learn more details about the various functions of the church *within* the new creation. As we soon notice, many of the features found in Revelation 22:1-5 remind us of Eden in Genesis 1–2. We have the presence of God, water, and the tree of life. But something is different. This is Eden to the max. In Genesis 1–2, God did indeed dwell with Adam and Eve, but his full presence remained in heaven. Here, though, "God and . . . the Lamb" dwell with humanity in their fullness. Every inch of the cosmos is nourished and filled with the presence of God.

Creation, too, is different. In Eden there was a single tree of life (Genesis 2:9), whereas in the new creation there are two trees of life, one on either side of the river (Revelation 22:2). Eternal life that was originally promised to Adam and Eve in the garden upon perfect obedience has been achieved through Christ's work and is now available to all who identify with him.

In the original creation, God ruled mightily over the created order, but he did so from heaven. This is one of the reasons why he created humanity in his image—to image him on earth by reflecting and refracting his rule. In the new heaven and earth the great gulf that separated God from his people has been removed. He rules exhaustively *over* the entire cosmos and from *within* it. If God's rule is so pervasive and comprehensive, will there no longer be a need for humanity to function as his images in the new creation? Will we cease functioning as kings, priests, and prophets?

Revelation 22 goes on to explain that nothing could be further from the truth. According to Revelation 22:3-4, "The throne of God and of the Lamb will be in the city, and his servants will serve him. They will see his face, and his name will be on their foreheads." Taken together, "servants serving him," "seeing his face," and bearing "his name on their foreheads" underscore the believers' role as high priests in the new creation (cf. Revelation 7:15). Just as priests served or worshiped in the physical temple (e.g., Numbers 16:9; Hebrews 8:5), so now the people of God will serve and worship in the new creation.

In the Old Testament, priests ministered in the temple by tending the lampstand, offering up incense, preparing the bread, and so on. Remember that priests in the Old Testament represent the entire people of God; they are the "firstborn" of the covenant community (Numbers 3:41). So, when priests ministered before the Lord in the physical temple in the Old Testament, their actions anticipated the day in which all of God's people would minister in the true, cosmic sanctuary of the new heavens and earth. Revelation 22:4 goes on to relate how each person in the new creation will "see his face, and his name will be on their foreheads." In the Old Testament, only the high priest bore God's name on his forehead. The writing on the plate was engraved with the words: "HOLY TO THE LORD" (Exodus 28:36). Only the high priest could enter into the holy of holies once a year, and when they did, they still had to offer up incense that created a buffer between them and God. Every believer has continuous and intimate access to God's presence for all of eternity! Humanity will finally see the face of God, an experience that even Moses did not enjoy (Exodus 33:20).

What does it mean concretely that we will worship and serve God in the new creation as high priests? Though I take much of Revelation 22:1-5 as symbolic (I doubt that we will have God's name literally on our foreheads), there are true spiritual realities behind the symbols. I do think that believers will function as high priests in the physical new earth. As I mentioned, priests in the Old Testament maintained the physical temple and kept all impurities outside of God's presence. In the new creation, all that is impure or unclean cannot penetrate the new cosmos. So what will we do? Though the Bible isn't explicit here, perhaps we can read between the lines a bit.

As high priests in the new earth, we will first and foremost worship the triune God. We, like the angels in Revelation 4–5, praise God for his holiness, his redemption, and his unrivaled rule. Another area in which we may function as priests is taking care of the new earth. In Eden, Adam and Eve were charged with caring for creation (Genesis 2:15). I wonder, then, if we will have a similar role. Certainly, the entire earth is one gigantic Eden (Revelation 22:1-2), but that does not preclude us from managing and harnessing it.

Take, for example, the basic issue of food. Will we eat in the new creation? Will Chick-fil-A be there? Since Jesus' glorified body is the prototype of our resurrected body (1 Corinthians 15:49), then it makes sense that we would eat in the new earth. The Gospels oddly point out that Jesus ate after his resurrection (Luke 24:30-43; John 21:10-14). *If* we eat in the new earth, then where will all the food come from? Unless manna falls from the sky, humanity, as priests, will be in charge of harvesting and preserving it. That will be no simple task. Every aspect of life in the new creation, no matter how mundane or profound, will be part of working and worshiping in God's cosmic temple. Our identity as priests will always be on display.

Perhaps another dimension of imaging God in the new creation will be the development of technology and science. Will we invent the wheel again? Will we learn how to start a fire once more? What about basic human knowledge such as math, language, music, and so on? I suspect that we will not start from scratch. One could possibly argue that we, being perfected in God's image, will develop what we learned in the past. The knowledge that humanity has acquired and is acquiring through observing the world around us may not only inform us about God's creative power, but it may also prepare us for life in the new creation. According to Revelation 21:24, "the nations will walk by its light, and *the kings of the earth will bring their splendor into it*." Here John claims that the prophecy of Isaiah 60:3-5, an oracle that describes the influx of the nations to Israel, will be ultimately fulfilled in the new creation. It may not be a stretch to envision that each people group will bring its own unique knowledge of the world into the new heavens and earth. Anthony Hoekema follows this line of reasoning:

> The best contributions of each nation will enrich life on the new earth, and that whatever potentialities and gifts have been of value in this present life will somehow, in some way, be retained and enriched in the life to come. This implies that there will be continuity as well as discontinuity between the present life and the life to come, and that therefore our cultural, scientific, educational, and political endeavors today help us to prepare for a fuller and richer life on the new earth.[4]

Certainly, the new creation will be different and our glorified bodies will be different, so the physical rules of the cosmos will probably be different too. Nevertheless, it's worthwhile to ponder these things.

---

[4]Anthony A. Hoekema, *Created in God's Image* (Grand Rapids: Eerdmans, 1986), 95.

KINGS IN THE NEW CREATION

We will serve in the new earth as priests, and we will rule in the new creation as kings. At the end of John's final vision, we read "and they will reign for ever and ever" (Revelation 22:5). The kingly dimension of being in God's image is explicit. John alludes here to a key passage in the book of Daniel: "Then the sovereignty, *power and greatness of all the kingdoms under heaven will be handed over to the holy people* of the Most High. His kingdom will be *an everlasting kingdom*, and all rulers will worship and obey him" (Daniel 7:27). John therefore claims that Daniel 7:27 is fully fulfilled in the new creation. Yes, this passage was initially fulfilled in the first coming of Christ, when believers "began" to rule, but here in Revelation 22 it's fulfilled in its all its fullness.

Much of Revelation draws attention to the book of Daniel, especially the Son of Man's enthronement in Daniel 7. Christ, as the Son of Man, promises believers that, if they do not succumb to idolatry, then they will sit with him on his throne (Revelation 3:21). Christ assures believers that they will mediate his rule and inherit the new earth. All believers remain in the image of God and will function as kings as they reign with him over the new earth. Indeed, our image will be completely restored at our resurrection, so that we will reign with Christ. His rule over the cosmos will flow through us. We will rule on his behalf, just like Adam and Eve were to rule on behalf of the Lord in the garden.

What does this reign look like? Is there hostility in the new creation that requires subjection? Revelation 21:1 states that there is "no longer any sea" in the new heaven and earth. The sea, in the Bible, symbolizes hostility and rebellion (e.g., Ezekiel 32:2; Daniel 7:2). Since there is no sea in the new earth, figuratively speaking, then there will be no shred of hostility against God or his people (cf. Revelation 21:8). If there is neither wickedness nor rebellion in the new creation, then what do believers rule over? The answer can be somewhat tricky. On one level, the New Testament claims that believers will rule over the angels in the new earth (1 Corinthians 6:3), so there is some element of creation that we will administer.

One facet of Adam's rule is his management of the animals. Just as God executed his kingly rule in naming the cosmos in creation, so too Adam functioned in the image of God by naming the animals (Genesis 2:20).

Adam and Eve were to employ their kingly status by extending God's rule on earth, especially over the animals. Though Revelation 21–22 does not explicitly mention animals dwelling in the new creation, I find it hard to believe that they will not be there. The animals are a constitutive part of the original creation and are mentioned repeatedly in Old Testament oracles that pertain to harmony within the new creation (e.g., Isaiah 11:6; 65:25). The Bible is filled with reminders about how God cares for the animals (Genesis 8–9), and the apostle Paul claims that "the *whole* creation has been groaning" for its long-awaited restoration (Romans 8:22). If animals dwell in the new earth, then we will probably rule over them and manage them in accordance with our kingly status. Perhaps this means that we will organize them, enjoy them, and work with them. Do all dogs go to heaven? Maybe.

PROPHETS IN THE NEW CREATION

Admittedly, the prophetic dimension is not as prominent here in Revelation 21–22 as our kingly and priestly dimensions. But I do think we can find traces of it. One avenue of exploration is to examine who will *not* participate in the new earth: "But the cowardly, the unbelieving, the vile, the murderers, the sexually immoral, those who practice magic arts, the idolaters and all liars—they will be consigned to the fiery lake of burning sulfur. This is the second death" (Revelation 21:8). These traits generally stem from two issues: a corrupted image and abusing God's images. The corrupted image, that is, a person who is unwilling to repent and trust in Christ, is labeled "cowardly," "unbelieving," "vile," "those who practice magic arts," "idolaters," and "liars." This individual is the opposite of an "overcomer" in Revelation (see Revelation 2:7, 11, 17; 3:5, 12; 5:5). An overcomer holds fast to Christ and perseveres in the face of persecution, whereas this person capitulates to temptation and relishes it. Like Adam and Eve succumbing to temptation in the garden and thus beginning to embody the characteristics of the serpent, this individual falls prey to temptation and takes on the nature of the devil.

The persons described here in Revelation 21:8 are also abusers of the divine image. Instead of treating one another with respect and living all of life in accordance with God's will, these people murder, commit sexual immorality, and lie to one another. Quite simply, the vice list here in Revelation 21:8 is a description of an anti-image. These people are attempting to live independently of God and cast off their divine image. They want to be God and usurp his role as Creator and sovereign ruler. They want to rule, but not on behalf of God. They want to be worshiped by God instead of worshiping God. They want to create truth instead of embodying the truth of God and communicating it to others. Only those who trust in Christ and resist idolatry will become part of God's family and inherit the new creation.

In the new earth, the entirety of our lives will be pleasing to God. We will embody his will and think his thoughts after him. We will speak nothing but truth to one another. We will love God more intensely than we do now. We will care for each other more tenderly.

One strand that's woven throughout the entire Bible is the importance of God's people recalling his wondrous acts of redemption. We know God because he reveals himself in his mighty acts. Israel's annual feasts were rehearsals of God's past redemption. The psalms are filled with the Israelites' praise of God for delivering their ancestors from Egypt and their anticipation of the day when he would do so again with great finality. Even the hymns within Revelation reflect on God's past and future redemption of his people. I wonder, then, if we will continue to recall God's redemption in the new creation. Perhaps the various communities that are scattered throughout the new earth will break out in song and joyously praise God for his work in his Son and Spirit. Perhaps we will scour the earth in search for the prophets of the Bible and ask them to recount God's work in their lives. The more we listen to the testimony of redemption by the people of God, the more we desire to exalt his name and bring him glory.

Fundamentally, images are created to promote not themselves but God, whom they represent. An easy way for us to discern whether our lives are pleasing to God is to ask whether our thoughts and actions honor God or ourselves. If our actions are consonant with God and his will as revealed in the Bible, then we are glorifying God. If we are acting out of our own self-interest, then we are attempting to cast off his image and be God.

CONCLUSION AND APPLICATION

What makes the book of Revelation so fascinating is its presentation of the people of God. On the one hand, John's depiction of the community of faith is sobering and difficult to swallow. Revelation 14:4 puts it so aptly: "They follow the Lamb wherever he goes." All believers, just like the Lamb they follow, will eventually be overcome by the world in some fashion—physically, emotionally, financially, and so on. We should expect nothing but hostility on all fronts.

On the other hand, John dedicates much material to depicting the church in the new creation. Indeed, the final vision is the climax of the book. The vision assures the suffering church on earth that their future is bright. God will bring to completion what he promised long ago in the Garden of Eden—dwelling intimately with his people in the new creation. N. T. Wright captures the thrust of Revelation when he argues,

> It is the final answer to the Lord's Prayer, that God's kingdom will come and his will be done on earth as in heaven. It is what Paul is talking about in Ephesians 1:10, that God's design, and promise, was to sum up all things in Christ, things in heaven and on earth. It is the final fulfillment, in richly symbolic imagery, of the promise of Genesis 1, that the creation of male and female would together reflect God's image in the world. And it is the final accomplishment of God's great design, to defeat and abolish death forever.[5]

How does our future motivate us today? We need to fall into the rhythm of the new creation. Since all those who are in Christ are a new creation (2 Corinthians 5:17), we are beginning to reap the benefits of the new cosmos. The physical and spiritual restoration of God's people and creation that the Old Testament prophets envisioned at the very end of the age has been applied to the saints. Believers are not only forgiven through faith in Christ; they are also created anew by God's end-time Spirit. We must love, serve, worship, and live righteously here and now, so that when we are raised fully and planted in the new cosmos, we will *continue* to do what we already started. We must develop new creational patterns of living in the present.

---

[5]N. T. Wright, *Surprised by Hope: Rethinking Heaven, the Resurrection, and the Mission of the Church* (San Francisco: HarperOne, 2008), 105.

RECOMMENDED READING

Alexander, T. Desmond. *The City of God and the Goal of Creation.* Wheaton, IL: Crossway, 2018.

Middleton, J. Richard. *A New Heaven and a New Earth: Reclaiming Biblical Eschatology.* Grand Rapids: Baker Academic, 2014.

Wright, N. T. *Surprised by Hope: Rethinking Heaven, the Resurrection, and the Mission of the Church.* San Francisco: HarperOne, 2008.

Chapter Twelve

CONCLUDING PRACTICAL REFLECTIONS

IMAGE LEADS TO IDENTITY, and identity leads to behavior. We've discovered that God's people enjoy a rich identity yet incredible responsibilities as kings, priest, and prophets. God created us to image him on the earth and rule on his behalf, enjoy and mediate his presence, and proclaim and embody his truth. I've attempted to make concrete application of these precious truths throughout this project, but my goal here is to offer a few additional, albeit brief, reflections.

THE CHURCH AS TRUE ISRAEL

The church falls in continuity with the people of God throughout the history of redemption. We are not an aberration or a parenthesis in God's program. The story of the people of God in the Old Testament is our story. Abraham is *our* father. Indeed, he is a closer father than our biological father (see Mark 3:34)! When we read the Old Testament we should do so not as observers but as participants. One of the hallmarks of dispensationalism is to drive a wedge between Israel and the church. But such a move runs counter to so much of what we discover in the New Testament. There is one people of God spanning both Testaments. As we remind ourselves of who we are in Christ, we must do so in light of what the Bible says in the Old Testament as well as the New.

IMAGE AND MEANING

Since God is intent on restoring our minds and our bodies, what we do with them matters to him. We live in a post-Enlightenment era, and Western culture has attempted to erase all inklings of God. When it comes to our bodies, the spiritual and the physical are pitted against each other. Our culture contends that there is no spiritual but only physical. Since there is no God, there is no larger plan, no purpose, no goal, and, ultimately, no meaning. Modern culture attempts to find meaning and significance apart from being created in God's image, but the opposite is true—there is no meaning and significance without God. Psalm 139:14 reads,

> I praise you *because* I am fearfully and wonderfully made;
>   your works are wonderful,
>   I know that full well.

The church must respond by teaching and concretely demonstrating what it means to be in the image of God. Do we value life? Do we value marriage? Do we value our children? What about the poor and the outcast? The image of God and significance go hand in hand. Representing God on the earth is not oppressive but liberating. Living as a child of God in the perfected image of Christ is simply how we are created to function.

RULING WELL: KINGS

The fall did not destroy the image of God, but it did pervert it. Instead of ruling well, humanity is now prone to abusing one another and the created order. We are created to rule on behalf of God on the earth, but outside of Christ we have a proclivity toward exploitation, violence, and abuse. The West is becoming more aware of these issues in our culture, but it doesn't quite know how to remedy the situation. Our society knows, at least at some level, that all forms of abuse are wrong, but it doesn't know what to do about it. Enact better laws? The church has a wonderful opportunity here: show the world how to rule well. Instead of exploiting each other, we must treat one another with dignity and respect. Instead of letting sin rule over us, we must rule over sin. Our lives must be attractive to the world, full of contentment and righteousness.

WORSHIPING GOD ALONE: PRIESTS

Unbelievers are marked by worshiping everything except the triune God. Idol worship, figurative and literal, is natural for unbelievers. What characterizes God's people, though, is exclusive worship of him. God created us for *his* glory—not to glorify ourselves, our possessions, or our accomplishments. The world should see the church as utterly distinct in its worship. Why should unbelievers be attracted to Christianity if we worship and adore the same things? We must make it clear that the church is more than another social club. We are the people of God, and we worship none other.

EMBODYING GOD'S LAW: PROPHETS

In postmodern cultures, which devalue all forms of truth claims, believers must vigorously swim against the rising tide. The serpent tempted Eve in the garden by testing the veracity of God's law. We must not fall prey like our predecessors in the garden and treat God's Word lightly. He means what he says. The Bible informs God's people of who he is, of his commitment to dwell with us, and of how to navigate this difficult world as those who bear his image. O that the psalmist's words would ring true in our own hearts:

I rejoice in following your statutes
as one rejoices in great riches. (Psalm 119:14)

We talk about what we prize the most. Do we talk about the Bible like we talk about sports? Do we spend more time watching ESPN than we do digging into the Scriptures? There's nothing wrong with enjoying hobbies and recreation—indeed, we are fashioned to do so!—but we must treasure God's Word more. The Bible is a storehouse of riches, and as prophets created in the divine image, we should be filled with excitement to learn more about our Lord.

AUTHOR INDEX

SCRIPTURE INDEX

Finding the Textbook You Need

The IVP Academic Textbook Selector
is an online tool for instantly finding the IVP books
suitable for over 250 courses across 24 disciplines.

---

ivpacademic.com
